VISUAL QUICKSTART GUIDE

iMOVIE '09 & iDVD

FOR MAC OS X

Jeff Carlson

 Peachpit Press

Visual QuickStart Guide

iMovie '09 & iDVD for Mac OS X

Jeff Carlson

Peachpit Press

1249 Eighth Street
Berkeley, CA 94710
(510) 524-2178
(510) 524-2221 (fax)

Find us on the Web at: www.peachpit.com
To report errors, please send a note to errata@peachpit.com
Peachpit Press is a division of Pearson Education

Editor: Valerie Witte
Production Editor: Cory Borman
Composition: Jeff Carlson
Copyediting: Liane Thomas
Proofreading: Valerie Witte
Illustrations and photos: Jeff Tolbert, Laurence Chen, Jeff Carlson
Indexer: Ann Rogers

ISBN-13: 978-0-321-60132-2

ISBN-10: 0-321-60132-7

9 8 7 6 5 4 3 2 1

Printed and bound in the United States of America

Dedications:

To Leonard, whose one-month film class at Whitworth instilled in me an appreciation of movies beyond mere popcorn entertainment.

To my sister Lisa, ever encouraging and cheerful.

Special Thanks to:

Valerie Witte, for being on top of things while I focused on working through the manuscript.

Liane Thomas, for not hesitating to jump into the project when asked, and for her razor-sharp editing eyes.

Ann Rogers, for not only delivering a top-notch index but also sending little encouraging notes as we went along.

Cory Borman, for his quiet production expertise.

Laurence Chen and **Gena Morgan,** who provided the photos for the lighting examples in Chapter 4.

Jeff Tolbert, for updating my embarrassing line drawings of computer and video equipment, and for creating the lighting renderings in Chapter 4.

Don Sellers, for getting me up to speed with shooting, lighting, sound, composition, and providing a real-world reference.

Derick Mains, Paul Towner, Keri Walker, Janette Barrios, Khyati Shah, and **Theresa Weaver** at Apple for answering my questions and providing resources when I needed them.

Glenn Fleishman and **Kim Ricketts** (plus the various **long-distance inhabitants from earlier office incarnations**) at the Fremont nook for being the best reasons to go to the office. They're good inspiration and reassurance that this freelance thing actually works.

Susan Rimerman and **Becky Morgan** for providing last-minute assistance before the book went to press.

Nancy Aldrich-Ruenzel, Gary-Paul Prince, and even some non-hyphenated folks like **Cliff Colby, Sara Jane Todd, Scott Cowlin,** and **Paula Baker** at Peachpit Press.

Ellie Carlson, who is the world's most adorable model for her dad's video testing.

And, of course, **Kim Carlson,** who never hesitates to ask, "How can I help?" and keeps me inspired to do what I do each day (and who wrangles a garden into beautiful submission better than anyone I know).

TABLE OF CONTENTS

TABLE OF CONTENTS

Introduction

I was at Macworld Expo when Apple introduced the first version of iMovie, and seeing it in person was a bona fide "aha" moment for me and most of the people in attendance. Video editing, a skill that people spend years mastering in specialized schools, had arrived on the average user's Mac. *Of course* this was going to work. When Steve Jobs presented a short video of two children playing, I knew the days of long, choppy, uncdited videotape recordings were coming to a close. Not only can you easily—let me repeat that: *easily*—capture video footage and transfer it to your computer, you can now edit out all the bad shots, the awkward moments, and those times when the camera was inadvertently recording while dangling at your side.

Now, in 2009, Apple has helped redefine the whole notion of home movies. With built-in support for the high-definition HDV and AVCHD video formats (as well as widescreen digital video and native MPEG-4 formats), iMovie '09 gives you the chops to make your own independent feature film without appearing as if you made it in your basement—even if that's exactly what you did.

And when you're done editing the movie, send it to iDVD to create a professional-looking DVD that can play on most home DVD players. Your friends and family will be the ones saying, "Aha!"

Who should read this book

iMovie '09 & iDVD for Mac OS X: Visual QuickStart Guide is aimed at the beginning or intermediate videographer who wants to know how to edit movies quickly and easily in iMovie and create DVDs using iDVD. Perhaps you've just purchased your first camcorder and want to turn your home movies into little masterpieces, but don't have the time or money to invest in a professional video editing application. Or maybe you're an old hand at shooting video but new to editing the footage on a computer. Then again, maybe you're a budding Spielberg with scripts in your head and a passion for telling stories on film—the movie business is a tough one to crack, but it's entirely possible that your iMovie-edited film could be the springboard for a career in Hollywood. (In fact, one of the official entries at the 2004 Sundance Film Festival was edited in iMovie.) Or you could also be the owner of a new Mac, and want to know why Apple is going to the trouble of giving you a powerful video editing application *for free*.

Since iMovie's introduction, we've seen a boom in digital video editing. Sure, it was possible before, using much more complicated and expensive programs such as Final Cut Pro or Adobe Premiere (and you can still take that route). But with iMovie and iDVD, *anyone* can make a movie and burn it to a disc that can be played in nearly any consumer DVD player.

What's new in this edition

iMovie '09 adds many new features, many of which seemed oddly missing from iMovie '08. I've extensively updated Chapter 10 to include new capabilities such as the Precision Editor, image stabilization, and cutaways. I've also written a new chapter, "Themes and Maps," that covers those two new features.

Perhaps the biggest change, however, deals with the program that didn't change at all: iDVD. To keep the book's size (and cost) reasonable, I've removed the chapters that go into detail about working in iDVD and replaced them with a new "iDVD at a Glance" chapter.

But don't think that material is gone! I've made the iDVD section of the book available as a free download at `www.peachpit.com/imovieidvdvqs/` after you register your book.

An iMovie and iDVD toolbox

A full-size movie crew can be unbelievably large and take up a city block. You probably won't require that much gear, but a few items are necessary to use iMovie and iDVD.

◆ **Mac OS X 10.5.6 or later.** iMovie '09 and iDVD run under Apple's now and future operating system, Mac OS X, version 10.5.6 or later. You also need a Mac with an Intel processor, a Power Mac G5 (dual 2.0 GHz or faster), or iMac G5 (1.9 GHz or faster).

◆ **iMovie '09 and iDVD.** If you've purchased a Mac sometime after January 2009, you probably have iMovie '09 and iDVD already—look in the folder named *Applications*. The programs are also available as part of the $80 iLife '09 package, which includes iPhoto '09, Garage-Band '09, and iWeb '09.

◆ **A digital camcorder.** This handy and compact device records the raw footage you will edit in iMovie. If you own a camcorder that's not digital, you can still import video into iMovie using a third-party analog-to-digital converter. That said, I can't stress how much easier it is to work when you have a digital camcorder.

◆ **Lots of hard disk space.** Storage is getting cheaper by the day, which is a good thing. You'll need lots. I don't mean a few hundred megabytes tucked away in a corner of your drive. Realistically, if you don't have at least 10 GB (gigabytes) of storage (on the low side) to use for iMovie and iDVD, shop for a bigger hard drive.

The moviemaking process

Creating a movie can be a huge spectrum of experience, but for our purposes I'm going to distill it as follows.

1. **Preproduction.** If you're filming a scripted movie (with actors, sets, dialogue, etc.), be sure you hire the actors, build the sets, write the script, and otherwise prepare to shoot a film. On the other hand, if you're shooting an event or vacation, preproduction may entail making sure you have a camcorder (see Chapter 1), its batteries are charged, and that you have enough tape available.

2. **Capture footage.** With preproduction out of the way, it's time to actually film your movie. The shooting part is when this book starts to come in handy. Chapters 2 through 5 discuss methods of composing your shots, lighting the scenes, and capturing audio.

3. **Import footage into iMovie.** Your tape is full of raw video waiting to be sculpted by your keen eye and innate sense of drama. The next step is to import it onto your computer and into iMovie. See Chapter 8.

4. **Edit your footage in iMovie.** Before iMovie, average folks had no simple way to edit their footage. The result was endless hours of suffering as relatives were forced to watch every outtake, flubbed

shot, and those 10 minutes of walking when you thought the camera was turned off. iMovie changes all that. See Chapter 6 for a quick overview, and then delve into Chapters 7 through 15 to learn how to edit your video and audio, plus add elements such as transitions and titles.

5. **Export video.** The movie is complete, and it's a gem. Now you need to share it with the world. Using the information found in Chapters 16 through 18, you can share it with other Apple programs (like iDVD) and devices such as the iPhone, iPod and Apple TV, upload it to the Web, or export it to a QuickTime movie for downloading or further manipulation.

The DVD creation process

iDVD provides a clear path to customizing the appearance of your DVD, adding more content, and burning the DVD disc.

Chapter 19 provides an overview of how iDVD works, including choosing a theme and building a slideshow.

When it's time to burn a DVD, turn to Chapter 20 to choose an encoding method and burn your disc, or create a project archive that can be moved to another computer for burning there (such as a faster Mac).

This book's companion Web site

I maintain a frequently updated iMovie blog that includes additional tips, pointers to software, examples from the book, and other iLife-related information. Check often at http://www.jeffcarlson.com/imovievqs/.

What You Can Accomplish by the End of this Book

To say, "Prepare your acceptance speech" would be exaggerating a bit, but theoretically, you can use iMovie to create a feature film, award-winning documentary, or even just the best darn vacation video you've ever seen. As you delve deeper into digital video and nonlinear editing (NLE), you'll realize that more options and more control can be had with more sophisticated (and pricey) systems, such as Final Cut Express and Final Cut Pro. But nothing says you can't do what you want with iMovie.

Stepping out of the clouds, you should easily (there's that word again) be able to shoot, edit, and distribute your movie. In the process, you'll find a new respect for film and video—you can't help it. After using iMovie for a few hours, you'll start watching television with a new eye that picks up aspects like pacing, framing, transitions, and audio you may never have noticed before.

That's been my experience, and now look at me: I've written seven editions of this book. And assembled some of the best darn vacation movies you've ever seen.

Part 1
Shooting

THE DIGITAL CAMCORDER

Ages ago, my copy of iMovie 1.0 sat neglected on my hard drive for months because I had no easy way to import video footage. I could have used an analog-to-digital converter to bring in the contents of old videotapes (see Chapter 8), but it would have been a hassle. What I needed was a digital camcorder.

Although digital camcorders cost more than analog models, you can get a good quality model these days for less than $200. You can also easily spend $5,000 or more, with plenty of models falling between those ranges.

iMovie '09 gives you another option: high-definition (HD) digital camcorders that capture video at a much higher resolution. Prices range from about $200 for simple models to thousands of dollars, with most consumer-focused HD cameras hitting the $600-$900 range.

For the money, you get a host of features—and gimmicks. If you've not yet purchased a digital camcorder, this chapter will help you decide which combination of features is right for you. Note that I'll give some examples, but won't be recommending any particular model, because (like all technology) the field changes pretty quickly. If you already own a camcorder, skim this chapter to see which features are important and which you should turn off.

You May Already Own a Camcorder

That little point-and-shoot digital camera tucked into your pocket? Chances are, it can record video as well as shoot still photos. Lots of mid-range "super-zoom" cameras also shoot video, and even digital SLRs (single-lens reflex cameras, the ones that feature interchangeable lenses) are beginning to include video capture features.

Currently, however, video is mostly a tacked-on feature of most still cameras, which is why you should consider buying a dedicated camcorder if you're going to be doing more than just casual video shooting.

Buying a Camcorder

Here's a look at the important characteristics of digital camcorders.

HD or DV format

iMovie offers you an important choice: Should you shoot in standard DV (digital video, also sometimes referred to as SD, or standard definition), or in HD (high-definition video)?

Prior to 2004, shooting in HD required expensive cameras costing tens or hundreds of thousands of dollars. Now, you can get an HD camcorder for less than $500 (**Figure 1.1**).

HD video captures more image information than standard DV, and comes in three variations (**Figure 1.2**): *720p* measures 1,280 by 720 pixels, and captures each frame in its entirety (known as "progressive" capture, the "p" in 720p); *1080p* measures 1,920 by 1,080 pixels; and *1080i* measures 1,920 by 1,080 pixels, and interlaces each frame (hence the "i"; see **Figure 1.3**). HD also shoots in a 16:9 widescreen aspect ratio. As you might expect, video shot with an HD camera looks great on an HD television.

iMovie supports high-definition formats that are designed to work on consumer hardware: HDV (High Definition Video) is a consumer-level version of HD that uses MPEG-2 compression; AVCHD (Advanced Video Codec High Definition) uses MPEG-4 compression and stores footage on removable memory cards or an internal hard drive on some models; some cameras, like the Flip MinoHD, output straight MPEG-4 files.

Other higher-quality HD formats exist for professional gear, but if you're capturing uncompressed 10-bit HD video (requiring around 500 GB per hour of footage), you're probably not using iMovie. (See Chapter 8 for HD storage requirements.)

Figure 1.1 Panasonic's HDC-SD100 high-definition camcorder costs less than $600 (street price).

DV: 720 by 480 pixels

HD 720p: 1,280 by 720 pixels

HD 1080i: 1,920 by 1,080 pixels

Figure 1.2 HD uses much more image information than standard DV video. Also note that HD features a 16:9 widescreen aspect ratio, while SD uses the television standard 4:3 ratio.

Progressive frame

Interlaced frame   *Next interlaced frame*

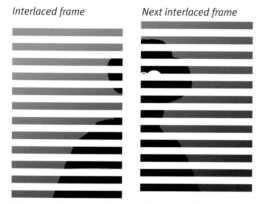

Figure 1.3 A progressive frame is captured in its entirety, the way each frame of film is recorded. Interlaced video captures every other line (exaggerated here for clarity) so that as the frames are played back, your eye sees the image as a solid picture. Interlacing can capture larger images because it's actually storing about half of the image information for each frame. (Interlacing is also the way most televisions operate.)

✔ Tips

- You need an Intel-based Mac to work with AVCHD footage in iMovie. However, if you're still using a Power PC-based Mac, a separate program called VoltaicHD (shedworx.com) can transcode the footage for later import into iMovie.

- To edit HD in its native resolution, you need a computer monitor at least 23 inches in size, such as Apple's Cinema Displays.

- iDVD handles incoming HD video, but it can't currently burn the HD-quality version to a disc. Even Blu-Ray DVD, which won the HD format war against HD-DVD, is currently not supported on the Mac. iDVD compresses the HD video to make it fit onto today's DVD media.

- The full scope of HD video production is enough to fill several books. For hands-on, in-the-trenches coverage of HD, I turn to *FreshDV* (www.freshdv.com). And don't forget the companion Web site for this book (jeffcarlson.com/imovie/).

BUYING A CAMCORDER

Tapeless camcorders

To make cameras even smaller, manufacturers are releasing cameras that store footage on flash memory (usually CompactFlash or SD cards, the type found in digital still cameras), smaller-sized DVD discs, and built-in hard drives. Most of the camcorders on the market now record to solid state memory, especially HD models using AVCHD. iMovie can import this footage (see Chapter 8), but the data is shrunk using MPEG-4 compression. That degrades the image quality, but you may not even notice (as described in the sidebar at right).

MiniDV tape format

If you don't need to shoot in HD and want to capture the best quality SD footage, get a camcorder that uses the MiniDV format (**Figure 1.4**). MiniDV tapes are compact, store 100 percent digital information, and record between 60 and 90 minutes of video. They're not particularly cheap, but they're not too expensive either.

MiniDV can store roughly 500 horizontal lines of resolution, which means you're capturing more information than other formats (televisions display about 330 lines). What's more, MiniDV tapes retain that quality when you record over them, or make copies from other MiniDV tapes.

That said, the writing is on the wall for MiniDV. Fewer camera models record to tape, and iMovie no longer supports writing edited footage back to tape.

✔ Tip

■ It doesn't matter which brand of MiniDV tape you choose—only that you stick with the same one. Companies use different lubricants on their tapes, so mixing brands can potentially lead to a sticky, camera-damaging mess.

Figure 1.4 As part of the miniaturization of digital camcorders, the tape media is smaller, too. But despite the size, MiniDV tapes store roughly one hour of high-quality video. HDV camcorders use the same tapes and store the same amount of footage.

Why Image Quality Is No Longer the Most Important Feature

Recording to tape provides the best image quality for SD video (HDV is written to tape, but stored as compressed MPEG-2 video). And yet, tapeless camcorders are selling in far greater numbers, despite the fact that those camcorders compress the footage and offer reduced image quality. Why the switch?

Convenience. Tape is linear, so you can't just jump to a particular scene without fast-forwarding or rewinding. It also requires that you import the footage in real time, making you wait an hour (for a typical full tape) before you can do any editing. As a result, a lot of tape ends up stacked on shelves or buried in drawers. For most people, it appears, the quality loss with tapeless formats is an acceptable trade-off.

I still subscribe to the notion that you want to start with the highest-quality image you can, but as the performance of AVCHD and other formats improves, I've turned a corner. Tapeless convenience has won out over image quality for me.

Figure 1.5 Today's digital camcorders are small enough to fit in your palm.

NTSC or PAL

Standard-definition video is broadcast in one of two formats, depending on where you live. In the Americas and many Asian countries, the standard is NTSC (National Television Systems Committee), which runs at 30 frames per second (actually 29.97 fps). In several European and some Asian countries, the standard is PAL (Phase Alternating Line), which runs at 25 fps. In most cases, you don't need to choose one or the other—you get whatever is predominant in your area. However, some people prefer to shoot in PAL because it's closer to the film projection rate of 24 fps. (Some camcorders now offer shooting in an optional 24 fps "cinema mode," but iMovie currently does not support it.)

Camcorder size

Ah, camcorder envy. You're carrying a new, tiny, handheld camcorder, but then you spy someone whose camcorder is even more compact. For those of us who've lugged shoulder-mounted VHS cameras back in the day, the miniaturization of camcorder technology is amazing. Although the majority of digital camcorders aren't super small, they're remarkable nonetheless—many fit into a large pants pocket or small purse (**Figure 1.5**).

The small sizes are ultra convenient, but have two drawbacks. Tiny camcorders have tiny sensors, so image quality might not be great. Also, a small camcorder that doesn't weigh much can be harder to keep steady when shooting. (iMovie's image stabilization feature can help; see Chapter 10.) If you're looking to grab footage anywhere and anytime, go as small as you can afford. If you anticipate more staged shots, where a camera can sit on a tripod for hours, size becomes less of an issue.

CCD and CMOS Sensors

A traditional movie camera records light onto a strip of film as it passes through the lens. In a digital camcorder, the light comes through the lens and is recorded by a CCD (charge-coupled device) or a CMOS (complementary metal–oxide–semiconductor), containing arrays of thousands or millions of tiny sensors that note the color of light striking them. When you put the sensors all together, they create the image you see on video.

Most camcorders come with a single sensor, varying in size and resolution, although some models feature three separate CCDs, each of which captures a specific color: red, green, or blue. You're not gaining any more image resolution, but the overall color quality is better than that offered by single-CCD cameras.

FireWire/i.Link and USB

As you'll soon discover, digital video data is massive, occupying about 3.6 MB *per second* for standard DV footage (see Chapter 8). Even a short movie would take forever to transfer from your camcorder to your Mac if not for the FireWire connection between the two (**Figure 1.6**). Also known on Sony camcorders as i.Link, FireWire is necessary to import movies from SD and HDV cameras into iMovie.

Tapeless camcorders increasingly use USB 2.0 ports, which offer about the same transfer speed as FireWire.

✔ Tip

■ If you use a USB hub to connect multiple devices to your Mac, make sure it's capable of USB 2.0 speeds.

Mac's FireWire port   Camera's FireWire/DV port

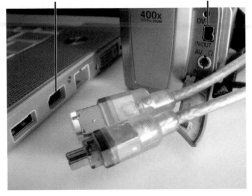

Figure 1.6 Use a high-speed FireWire connection to import your footage into iMovie on your Mac. You may need to purchase a cable like this one, which has both sizes of FireWire plugs.

The CMOS "Jelly Effect"

CMOS cameras record using what's called a "rolling shutter": the sensor captures image data from the top down. On some cameras, especially still cameras that shoot video, fast motion can cause the image to warp. Camcorders with CMOS sensors seem to handle the effect better. For an example, see: jeffcarlson.com/imovie/jelly.mov.

Figure 1.7 Canon's XL H1 is a high-definition MiniDV camera with all the trimmings. The microphone is mounted above the unit to record what you're shooting, not the sound of the camera itself.

Figure 1.8 An LCD viewfinder lets you shoot at odd angles. Rotate the screen to view the shot.

Microphone

Every digital camcorder has a microphone, usually built into the body of the camera, but sometimes mounted to the top or front of the camera (**Figure 1.7**). One thing to watch out for is where the microphone is housed: if it's too close to the camcorder's motors, it could pick up the sound of the camera operating (including the motors used for zoom control). Whenever possible, experiment with a few different camcorder models to check their audio output. You can also attach an external microphone to the camera. See Chapter 5 for more information.

LCD viewfinder

Most digital camcorders include a liquid crystal display (LCD) viewfinder that pops out from the side of the camera and shows you what the lens sees. LCDs vary in size, from 2.5 inches (diagonal) on up. You can use it in place of the built-in viewfinder—often advantageous when you need to hold the camera above your head or near your feet (**Figure 1.8**), or if you're filming yourself and want to make sure your head hasn't slipped out of frame. (On some newer camcorders, the LCD is the only way to see what you're shooting.) The LCD is especially useful when you want to review your footage, or show video to a few people looking over your shoulder. And you'll find it invaluable for fast-forwarding to the end of your footage on a MiniDV camcorder, to make sure you don't accidentally shoot over your existing video.

✔ Tip

■ Remember, it takes power to light up the LCD's pixels and backlighting. Using it often will drain your camera's batteries faster than using the built-in viewfinder. Some cameras now include a switch to turn off or reduce the LCD's backlight to conserve battery power.

BUYING A CAMCORDER

Electronic image stabilization

The software running a modern digital camcorder can help you stabilize your image and prevent the shaky footage associated with small handheld cameras. To do this, the camcorder uses an outer portion of the total image as reference, then compares movement of objects within the field of view to the outer area (**Figure 1.9**). If most of the image moves together, the software assumes the whole camera is moving instead of just the objects, and compensates by shifting the active image.

Electronic image stabilization is helpful, but certainly has its drawbacks. It doesn't record the entire screen, so in some cases you may find that objects on the periphery don't show up in the final footage. It's also not good if you're intentionally moving the camera, such as when you pan or zoom, because the software has to figure out that your motion is deliberate; the end result is sometimes blurry motion that would otherwise be clearer. Still, compared to footage that looks like it was shot during an earthquake, these trade-offs become more acceptable.

✔ Tips

- Of course, image stabilization isn't so good that it will make the shot you took while running down the street look like it was filmed with a Steadicam.

- iMovie's image stabilization feature can greatly improve shaky footage, even video shot with a camcorder that was using its own image stabilization technology. See Chapter 10 for more information.

Guide area

Image shifted, prompting the camera to compensate

Figure 1.9 In this *massively* simplified diagram, the original image (top) is shifted to the right (bottom) by the camera operator's nervousness around such towering animals. The camera compares the image to the pixels in the unrecorded guide area and compensates by shifting the main image to match. (In reality, the camera doesn't use such a huge guide area—it divides the entire image into several quadrants and continually compares each guide area to its corresponding image area.)

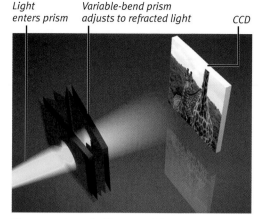

Light enters prism | Variable-bend prism adjusts to refracted light | CCD

Figure 1.10 An optical image stabilization system uses two lenses to detect light refraction.

Optical image stabilization

Another option for stabilizing your video is to buy a camera with *optical* image stabilization. Unlike the digital method, optical stabilization uses a prism composed of two lenses with silicon fluid between them. The prism determines whether the light coming into the lens is refracted (think of how a stick poking halfway out of water appears to bend below the water's surface). If it is, the camcorder adjusts the lenses to remove the refraction (**Figure 1.10**). An optical stabilizer can work a bit slower than an electronic stabilizer—since it's performing mechanical, not digital, adjustments—but tends to be a bit smoother overall.

Lens optics

The camera's lens is your eye to the footage you'll shoot, so optical quality is an important consideration. The lenses in the majority of cameras are of good quality, but more-expensive models tend to feature better optics. I'm not saying more-expensive lenses are always better, of course. But don't immediately assume that because a camera has a famous name written on its lens, the quality will be vastly better. Research different models and read owner reviews online to learn more.

Remote control

It's not like you don't have enough remote controls lying around the house. I thought having a remote control for a camera was a dumb idea until I realized its two main purposes: playing back video when the camera is attached to a television or monitor, and controlling recording when you can't be near the camera (such as when you're in the frame). The remote ends up being more important than I thought.

BUYING A CAMCORDER

Features Worth Noting

Electronics manufacturers love to make bulleted lists of features. Some you may never need or want, while others can help you improve the footage you shoot.

Focus

It's a safe bet that you want the subjects in your video to be in focus—but which subjects, and when? Camcorders feature automatic focus control, which is great when you're shooting footage on the fly. Who wants to try to manually focus when following animals in the wild (**Figure 1.11**)?

Figure 1.11 Gratuitous vacation footage inserted here. But really, when you're shooting video on the run, trying to focus manually at the same time would mean losing the shot. You can view this movie clip at jeffcarlson.com/imovie/focus.mov.

However, sometimes the automatic focus can be too good, bringing most objects in a scene into focus—which is why camcorders include an option for manually focusing the lens. (Higher-end models include a focus ring built around the lens, like on a DSLR still camera. Most smaller camcorders sport small dials or scroll wheels to control manual focus.) Manual focus is essential for some situations, such as interviews, when you're not moving the camera (see Chapter 2).

Shutter speed

The term "shutter speed" is a bit misleading here, since a digital camcorder doesn't technically have a shutter (a door or iris that opens quickly to allow light to enter the lens). However, it's possible to duplicate the effects of different shutter speeds by changing the setting on the camera. This is good for filming action with movement that would otherwise appear blurry (such as sporting events). Shutter speed is measured in fractions of a second, so a setting of 1/60 is slower than 1/8000 (see Chapter 3).

Normal

Low-light setting

Figure 1.12 Some camcorders feature a low-light setting, which boosts the effectiveness of the available light.

Night vision/low light

You have a few options for filming in low-light conditions. You could always carry around a full lighting setup, but that's not realistic. To compensate, some cameras include a night-vision mode that picks up heat from objects near the camera and displays a greenish representation of the scene.

Other cameras may include a low-light setting, which boosts the amount of available light that's picked up by the camera's image sensors (**Figure 1.12**). It's surprisingly effective, though the playback can be stuttered or blurry if a lot of movement is in the scene.

S-Video or HDMI port

All camcorders offer some type of output port so you can hook up a television or monitor to play back your footage. Usually, RCA-style plugs are included, but some models also offer an S-Video port. Hooking up your camera to a TV with an S-Video cable provides a clearer picture than with other AV cables. Use it if you've got it.

Modern high-definition televisions include one or more HDMI (High-Definition Multimedia Interface) ports, which enable you to connect one HDMI cable that transfers both video and audio. Some HD camcorders now include HDMI ports as well.

Features to Ignore/Avoid

Just as there are features you should pay attention to, some features should be ignored or outright avoided. Most of these are included for buyers who don't have the means to edit their movies after shooting. Most importantly, these effects permanently alter your footage, which you can't correct later in iMovie.

Figure 1.13 Digital zoom creates lots of pixelation as the camera tries to interpolate the image.

◆ **Digital zoom.** One of the first features you'll see on a camera is that it has a 200X (or higher) digital zoom. The technical interpretation is that the computer inside the camera digitally enlarges the image it's seeing, and it appears as if the camera is zoomed beyond its optical capabilities (**Figure 1.13**). The real-world interpretation, at least for now, is that some marketer somewhere is smiling and thinking about the wisdom of P.T. Barnum. Digital zoom isn't pure hokum, but it's also not a mature enough technology to be used in your movies. I expect that as cameras become more powerful and the image processing chips and software speed up (as they inevitably will), digital zoom will become a powerful tool. But not yet.

◆ **Special effects.** Before iMovie, you couldn't apply "sophisticated" techniques such as fade-in or fade-out without using an expensive professional editing system. So, camcorder makers added the capability to apply fades, wipes, and image distortions such as sepia tones or solarization (**Figure 1.14**). Well, forget special effects entirely—you can do them better in iMovie, with more control, and without degrading your footage.

Figure 1.14 In-camera special effects are really only good for ruining otherwise good footage. And not to sound mean, but the Mosaic (top) and Wave (bottom) effects shown here aren't even that interesting.

FEATURES TO IGNORE/AVOID

Date stamp

Created: Tuesday, March 7, 2006 11:59:00 AM

Figure 1.15 iMovie notes the date and time a clip was shot, so you don't need to use a date stamp feature that permanently adds it to the footage.

◆ **Date stamp.** You can optionally display the date and time on your footage, which would appear to be helpful if not for the fact that the information remains on the tape. Even with this feature disabled, your camcorder is recording (but not displaying) this data, which shows up in iMovie when you view information about a clip (**Figure 1.15**). Similarly, avoid built-in options for adding titles.

◆ **Still photo.** Most cameras now include the capability to take still photos. This is a good idea in theory, but the execution varies widely. Some cameras can capture progressive-scan images—which means every pixel is grabbed—and then save them to a separate memory card (such as SD or Sony Memory Stick cards). These result in better images, depending on the camera, but still not as good as what you'd get from most digital still cameras. A few models now include separate CCDs (and even separate lenses) to take higher quality images.

The technology is always improving, so it's possible that soon you may be able to buy a still photo and video camera combination that works well for both tasks. But personally, I'm more comfortable carrying two cameras that each excels at its appointed tasks.

COMPOSITION AND COVERAGE 2

Camcorder in hand, it's time to start shooting. Where to start? The easiest route is to point the lens at something and start recording. You're bound to get some good footage. However, by learning how to improve your video as you shoot it, you'll end up with better source footage when it's time to edit.

The material in this chapter (and the rest of the chapters in this section of the book) isn't rocket science. If you've grown up watching television or movies (as we all have, to varying degrees), some of it may be too obvious to warrant mentioning. And yet, when it comes time to shoot, it's all too easy to forget the basics and just let the camcorder run—again, perfectly acceptable, but you might kick yourself when you start working with your footage in iMovie. Remember, iMovie can help you edit your clips into a professional-looking movie, but it can't help you improve mediocre source material.

In this chapter, I'll touch upon the basics of getting a shot, and introduce you to some techniques for framing your scenes and shooting plenty of coverage to work with later. Depending on what you're shooting, some or all of this material may apply—you may have control over aspects such as lighting and how the subjects act, or you may be on safari trying to film elephants while avoiding getting eaten by lions.

Preproduction

In general, the term *preproduction* refers to everything done before the camera starts rolling. I think it's safe to assume that you know how to operate your camcorder, and you probably know roughly what you want to shoot. The following steps—except for the first one, which I consider essential—are optional, depending on the type of movie you're shooting. (For example, feel free to storyboard your baby's first steps, but she'll ultimately be the one to decide how that scene plays out.)

♦ **Imagine the end result.** Before you even turn on your camcorder, think about how the video will be seen. Will it be viewed on a television, movie screen, computer monitor, or maybe a combination of them all? This decision will help you when shooting. For example, if your movie will only appear on the Web, you may want to shoot more close-ups of people, to make sure they're identifiable in a small window on your computer screen. If it's going to be shown on a big-screen television, you could frame your shots with wider vistas or complex action in the shot.

♦ **Write the script.** If you're shooting a fictional story with scenes, sets, actors, and the like, you're going to need a script. Sure, the bigwigs in Hollywood don't always start movies with a script, but you've no doubt seen one of those stinkers and wondered if entire sections of Los Angeles underwent covert lobotomies. A good movie starts with a good script, without exception. Even in the low-budget world of digital video filmmaking, a good script can often overcome bland direction, lighting, staging, acting, sound, and so on.

An Afternoon, A Life

Shortly after starting work on the first edition of this book, I spent an afternoon with a colleague of mine, who also happens to be an Emmy-winning filmmaker, to pick his brain about filmmaking. "Anything in particular?" he asked me.

"Shooting, lighting, sound...," I replied.

He laughed. "Some people spend their entire lives learning just *one* of those skills."

Filmmaking is an evolutionary art, and involves far more than I can include in this book. I'll cover the basics, but I highly recommend consulting Appendix B for resources on where to learn more about shooting.

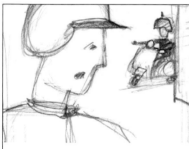

Figure 2.1 Drawing up a storyboard will help you visualize your shots and save time. If you're shooting casually or on the go, create a list of shots you want to try to capture. (Your storyboards are likely to run left-to-right, like most, but I'm working in a vertical layout here.)

◆ **Create storyboards.** Another step in producing a good fictional movie is creating storyboards: shot-by-shot sketches of what you want to shoot (**Figure 2.1**). In fact, you can use storyboards for documentary-style shooting, too. The point of storyboarding is to formulate your idea of what to shoot before you actually shoot; this process will save you time and help ensure that you're capturing all the visuals you want. At the very least, make a list of things you want to shoot, even if you're grabbing vacation video.

◆ **Prepare your equipment.** Do you have plenty of memory cards or MiniDV cassettes? Spare batteries—and are they charged? Power cord or battery charger? Lens cleaning cloth? Tripod? "Going to shoot video" can simply mean bringing your body and camcorder; or, it can involve hauling truckloads of equipment. In either case, make sure you have what you'll need to accomplish the job.

Understanding Timecode

Timecode is the measurement system for keeping track of where on a tape or in memory your footage is stored. DV and HDV camcorders use traditional timecode that recognizes individual frames. Many tapeless camcorders refer to the time in just hours, minutes, and seconds. (iMovie uses both formats; see Chapter 10.)

DV and HDV camcorders

As you shoot, you're recording video to the MiniDV tape. If you ever want to find that footage again, you need to understand timecode, the method camcorders use to label and keep track of footage.

As the tape advances, the camcorder notes precise points on the tape where footage is being recorded and displays a numeric tracking code in the viewfinder or on the LCD screen (**Figure 2.2**). A full timecode notation looks like this:

    01:42:38:12

The interpretation of those numbers is a lot like telling time on a digital clock, except for the last two digits:

    Hours:Minutes:Seconds:Frames

So, our timecode number above is read as 1 hour, 42 minutes, 38 seconds, and 12 frames. NTSC digital video records at 30 frames per second (fps), so the last number starts at :00 and ends at :29; for PAL video, which records at 25 fps, the range is between :00 and :24.

When you're recording, you typically won't see all of those numbers. More common is something like 0:03:31 (zero hours, 3 minutes, and 31 seconds), because the camera doesn't split out partial seconds (so no frame numbers are shown).

Timecode indicator

Figure 2.2 The camera assigns a timecode to each frame of film, which is used to manage your footage later in iMovie.

Timecode indicator

Figure 2.3 Some tapeless camcorders count video in hours, minutes, and seconds instead of in traditional timecode.

Tapeless camcorders

Tapeless camcorders record each scene as a separate element in memory (whether that's a memory card, DVD, or hard disk), so they don't use timecode. Instead, each clip starts at zero (**Figure 2.3**). (The original capture time is saved, however; in iMovie, choose View > Playhead Info, or press Command-I, to see this label.)

This situation isn't a problem in iMovie, since all clips appear as discreet items whose time markers begin at zero.

Shooting Video Without Disruption

I'm always a little self-conscious when I'm shooting, because often I have to make myself conspicuous in order to get the shot I want. On vacation, this isn't always a problem (my little camcorder is much less intrusive than that other guy's honkin' 35mm lens), but some occasions—for example, weddings—call for discretion. You can take a few different approaches to shooting without disruption.

For one, you don't have to shoot with the camera in front of your face. You can rotate the LCD screen and film from your hip (or even shoot behind you). If it's inevitable that your camera is going to be noticeable, don't be rude about it. People will understand if you need to step softly into view for a few seconds to get a shot, then retreat to a neutral location. Depending on the circumstances, try to ingratiate yourself into the scene so the people involved will trust that you won't be obnoxious.

Or, you could take the route of a professional still photographer who was on a recent vacation I took: Not only was he taking great pictures, he offered to sell the resulting photos to fellow vacationers. People (at least the ones whom I assume bought the album) no longer seemed to mind so much if he blocked their view.

Take Notes

When shooting, you may think you'll remember that the panda bears were located at roughly the 24-minute mark of the Panasonic tape with the purple label, but in reality you'll find yourself scanning through the footage and wishing you'd taken the time to take notes. Get a simple binder and make columns for the tape, timecode, and notes. Then, as you're shooting, jot down what you've just filmed. It doesn't have to be complicated, as long as it offers a quick reference to where your scenes occur. Taking notes is also essential when you need to keep track of locations and the names of people who appear in your video.

✔ Tips

- Label your tapes and memory cards. They add up quickly, tend to look alike, and are guaranteed to fall off your desk in a cluttered heap just before you need to grab the right one in a hurry.

- Listen, I hate taking notes, too. With digital video, however, you have an advantage: Before or after a shot, simply keep the camera running and speak your details. It won't help you find a clip in the middle of a tape, but it will give you the important details of what was recorded.

- Another suggestion is to use a few seconds of your video to record informative signs or other helpful visual indicators (**Figure 2.4**). You don't need to use this footage in your movie, but it helps as a reference when you're editing.

Footage for movie

Footage for reference

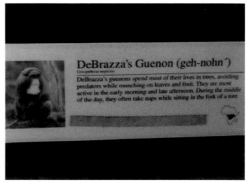

Figure 2.4 In lieu of keeping a notebook, take shots of signs or other identifying markers.

TAKE NOTES

Figure 2.5 Sweeping vistas don't always work in small movie windows, so try to shoot large when you can. Don't abandon wide shots, however. Tape is relatively cheap, so grab the shot when it's available; you can intercut the wider shots later when you're editing in iMovie. See "Coverage" later in this chapter.

Shooting Person A　　　　　　　　　*Axis*

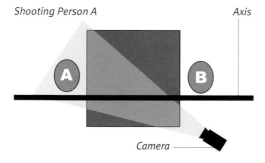

Camera

Shooting Person B

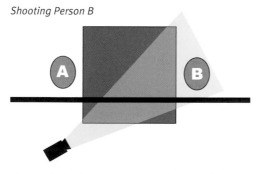

Figure 2.6 Keeping the camera on the same side of your axis line helps the viewer maintain a mental geography of the scene.

Composing Your Shots

If you really want to, you can hold the camcorder up in the air and hit record—with your eyes closed. But by putting a small amount of thought into the composition of your shots, you can give them a much more professional look.

Shoot large

I had the opportunity to see a 70mm print of *Lawrence of Arabia* a few years ago on the massive screen at Seattle's Cinerama theater. The movie is filled with sweeping desert vistas where you can see miles in every direction, taking full advantage of a large-screen experience.

Most likely, your video will instead play on a television screen or as a QuickTime movie on a Web page (**Figure 2.5**). For that reason, try to "shoot large"—make sure the subject is large enough in the frame that it's instantly recognizable even on a small screen. Getting closer also reveals more detail than can be seen from a distance.

Maintain an axis

Most people are fluent enough in the language of film that they aren't thrown by sudden cuts or changes in a scene. But visually crossing an axis tends to freak them out. The idea is this: if you have two people in a scene, and you're switching between close-ups of each one, they should both remain on their own sides of the screen (**Figure 2.6**). If character A is on the left side of the table, but then you move the camera so that he appears on the right side of the *screen*, the viewer is left wondering how he moved so quickly. At the very least, she'll notice that something odd has happened, which distracts her from the movie's content.

Balance your shots

As I look through some of my old still photos, I notice an annoying consistency: everything is centered. People, monuments, sunsets—all evenly positioned between the edges of the frame. Perhaps it's just our nature to center objects, but it's a good habit to break. Go watch television or a movie and you'll see that almost nothing is centered.

Positioning elements slightly askew of center makes them more interesting. Another take on this positioning is called the *rule of thirds*: the focus of your composition should appear one third of the way from the edge of the frame (**Figure 2.7**). Also make sure that the subject is facing into the frame, not toward the outside (**Figure 2.8**).

✔ Tips

■ As you're shooting, be aware of everything in your field of view—don't just focus your attention on the subject. If something else is distracting or disturbing elsewhere in the frame, viewers will likely gravitate toward that, and away from your subject.

■ Similarly, take your environment into consideration when possible. Because video is interlaced (every other horizontal line on the television screen is displayed), some objects, such as window blinds, may create distracting patterns onscreen.

■ Some camcorders can overlay a grid onto the viewscreen that divides the image into thirds and helps you level your shot (the grid doesn't appear in your video). Check your camera's manual to learn how to activate the feature.

Figure 2.7 The train's engine appears in the first third vertical portion of this shot.

Figure 2.8 When your subject faces toward the middle of the frame, he remains engaged with the rest of the shot, rather than looking outside the frame at something else (which is then where your viewers will want to look).

Figure 2.9 Camcorders do a good job of focusing—sometimes too good. In this shot, Greta is competing with the chair and the firepit in the background for the viewer's attention.

Figure 2.10 Objects in the foreground, such as the branches of this tree, can throw off your camcorder's automatic focus and obscure what you wanted to capture (in this case, a rhino in the wild).

Avoid Bouncing Video

If you're shooting a fixed object where the camera won't move (such as a person being interviewed), use manual focus. Sometimes the motion of the person talking (if they move forward slightly when making a point, for example) will trigger the camera to adjust its automatic focus, causing other elements in the frame to "bounce."

Focus

Pity the poor UFO watchers of days gone by, with their bulky cameras and—most distressingly—manual focus. It's hard enough to spot a saucer in the sky, but to also keep it in clear focus was a daunting task.

I suspect that today's sky-watchers are thrilled with modern camcorders, if for no other reason than the inclusion of *automatic focus control*. Thanks to millions of calculations processed while shooting, a camcorder can do an amazing job of keeping objects in focus. Sometimes, however, the camera performs its job too well.

Automatic versus manual focus

Digital camcorders use automatic focus by default. Although they include some sort of manual focus control (which is often a small dial that's hard to adjust in the middle of shooting), most likely it's not the type of focus ring found on your 35mm still camera. Nonetheless, don't be tempted to let automatic focus dominate your shots.

Auto focus tends to focus everything in view, causing footage to appear hyper-real at times (**Figure 2.9**). Your eyes don't bring everything into focus as you look around, so video that is predominantly focused can be distracting.

In an ironic twist, automatic focus can actually contribute to blurry images. The camera generally attempts to focus the objects in the foreground (which may appear on the periphery of the image and not be immediately visible to you), but that can throw off the focus in the rest of the shot and leave your subjects blurry (**Figure 2.10**).

If your camera is mostly stationary, experiment with manual focus to ensure that the objects you want to capture remain in focus.

Depth of Field

We usually want to keep things in focus, but when everything appears sharp, most scenes begin to look flat. Instead, highlight objects in the foreground by keeping them in focus, and separate them from the background by keeping it soft. When you decrease this depth of field, you're more effectively simulating how a viewer's vision works, and subtly influencing what they should see. This works particularly well during interviews or scenes where a character is occupying the frame.

To decrease depth of field:

1. Position the camera as far away from your subject as possible.

2. Use the camcorder's zooming controls to zoom in close to the subject.

3. Set the manual focus so that the subject is clear (**Figure 2.11**).

✔ Tip

■ Professional shooters achieve shallow depth of field by using interchangeable lenses with large apertures. Then again, they're not using consumer equipment. However, that ability may not be out of your reach. A growing number of DSLR (digital single-lens reflex) still cameras, such as the Nikon D90 and Canon 5D Mark II, can now record HD video. Shooting with an inexpensive 50mm lens with a maximum aperture of f/1.8 yields beautiful depth of field (**Figure 2.12**). These cameras aren't quite up to the task for casual shooting—automatic focus is an issue, for example—but the technology is quickly improving.

Figure 2.11 The background is out of focus and less vibrant compared to the foreground, which helps to visually separate the two.

Figure 2.12 This video was shot with a Nikon D90 DSLR using a 50mm f/1.8 lens to take advantage of a shallow depth of field.

Coverage

With some basics under your belt about framing your shots, we come to a bigger question: Which shots are needed to create a movie? If you're shooting a family event, you may think the question doesn't apply to you; after all, you shoot whatever happens, right?

Well, shooting the event itself is a good start, but you need more than that. And you need to make sure you have enough *coverage*, the footage that will give you plenty of room to work when you're editing in iMovie.

Shoot to edit

At the beginning of this chapter, I advised you to imagine the end result of your movie before you begin shooting. A similar notion is *shooting to edit*. In the days before anyone with a Mac could edit their movies, amateur filmmakers shot "in the camera," meaning they structured their shot process so that scenes fell sequentially in the order they would appear when the tape was played— "editing" was done in advance by planning what to shoot.

Now, you're shooting with the knowledge that your raw footage is going to be edited in iMovie. You don't have to shoot things in order, limit yourself to the main subject, or even use footage from the same session.

By way of example, suppose you're filming a family reunion. Immediately following the pick-up basketball game (where Uncle Barney surprised everyone with 32 points and a slam dunk), you shoot a few minutes of a woodpecker perched on a nearby tree. Then you return to the festivities. The woodpecker has nothing to do with the family reunion, so you may not even use it in your final video—or perhaps you'll pop a few seconds of it into the beginning to show what a beautiful, nature-filled location everyone enjoyed.

As another example, to round out your movie you want to show the sunset and then fade to black. Unfortunately, the sunset footage you shot wasn't as memorable as you remembered, so instead you grab 20 seconds of sunset footage you took on another location and insert that into your movie. Unless it's painfully obvious that the two locations are different (the presence of a sandy beach where before you were in the middle of a forest, for example), no one will know the difference, and your movie will end stronger. In each example, you had extra footage at your disposal because you were shooting to edit.

Types of coverage

When shooting a feature-length motion picture, a director will use multiple camera setups to shoot as much coverage as possible. So in one scene, the camera may shoot both actors in the frame, each actor from one or more different positions, and various combinations of points of view. The goal is to present a scene in the edited movie where the camera position is integral to the scene's mood or content.

◆ **Establishing shot.** This is usually an overview shot that's wide enough to let the viewer know the setting and which characters inhabit the scene (**Figure 2.13**). It can be a sign reading "Welcome to Twin Falls," a shot of someone's house, or a shot of a room. The important thing is that the establishing shot provides a physical geography of where objects appear. (This technique is used to great effect in dozens of movies and television shows: you see an establishing shot of the Chicago skyline and assume that the action takes place there, even though the actual filming took place in Vancouver.)

Figure 2.13 An establishing shot gives the viewer a sense of where the next scenes will occur, such as this shot of a campsite.

Figure 2.14 A medium shot is typically close enough to include two or three people.

Figure 2.15 A close-up focuses on one person or object that occupies most of the frame.

◆ **Medium shot.** Most shots end up as variations of medium shots. Generally, this shot is large enough to frame the torsos of two or three people, although it can vary between a shot of a single person or half of a room (**Figure 2.14**).

◆ **Close-up.** The screen is filled with part of a person or object (**Figure 2.15**). Close-ups usually show a person's head and shoulders, but can also push in closer (known as an extreme close-up) so you see only the person's eyes. Other examples of close-ups include shots of a person's hands, or any object that occupies the entire frame.

◆ **Cut-away shots.** Sometimes referred to as B-roll footage, cut-aways are shots of associated objects or scenes that aren't necessarily part of the central action in a scene. An example would be the view from a ship traveling through a passage, which cuts away to a shot of the darkening sky, then returns to the ship safely emerging from the passage. The woodpecker footage mentioned in the family reunion example earlier could easily be used as a cut-away shot. Cut-aways often prove invaluable when you need to cover up a few frames of a glitch or when cutting and shortening interviews.

◆ **In points and out points.** If possible, give yourself some shots that can be used to enter or exit a scene, sometimes known as in points and out points. For example, if you're shooting an interview and your subject has just declared his intention to walk on Mars, don't immediately stop recording. Hold the camera on him as he finishes speaking, then perhaps pan down to his desk where a model of his rocket ship is mounted.

✔ Tips

- Linger on shots when you can. It's far easier to cut out footage than to add it back in later (especially if it's vacation footage or something similar…unless you *really* need to rationalize a trip back!).

- How long should you hold on to a shot? First of all, don't automatically shut off the camcorder just when the action has stopped. Stay for a few seconds or minutes to let the emotion of a scene dissipate. This is true when you're doing interviews or shooting wildlife. You can always trim it later in iMovie.

- Remember that a camcorder isn't like a still camera. I've seen people rotate the camcorder 90 degrees as they would a still camera in an effort to shoot a "taller" image (**Figure 2.16**). Unfortunately, no matter how you shoot, the end result will still be a horizontal image—it's not a print that you can view vertically.

  (That said, your footage *can* be salvaged. See Chapter 10 to learn how.)

- Here's a tip I came across while on a soggy camping trip. When shooting in poor weather, you'll need to protect your gear. You can buy hoods and covers and other accessories, which are fine but add bulk and can be pricey. Instead, I have a fleece vest that I use to cover the camera: the lens points through one arm hole, protecting it from the rain but still giving enough room for me to operate the camera. I wouldn't use it in a downpour, but it's come in handy several times when the weather has been sketchy.

Figure 2.16 Resist the temptation to rotate your camcorder as you would a still camera to take "vertical" shots, because in video they'll look like this.

THE CAMERA IN MOTION

3

My digital camcorder is small enough that I can take it almost anywhere. While we're driving to work, my wife will occasionally grab the camera out of my bag and start shooting anything that catches her eye: a brilliant sunrise, the way Seattle's skyline materializes on a foggy morning, rows of orange-tipped trees alongside the roadway in the fall. Although we initially bought the camera to take with us on vacation, it has turned into an unofficial chronicler of our lives.

One of the advantages of a small camera is that it easily moves with you. However, when you're shooting, motion can become a character in its own right. Slowly moving across a scene imparts a different feeling than quickly scanning your surroundings, for example. This chapter addresses the most common ways of moving the camera to add motion to your movie, including the number one rule: Don't move.

Don't Move

It's time to go watch TV again (hey, this moviemaking stuff is easy!). Turn to a scripted dramatic show and note how often the camera moves. I don't mean how often the *camera is moved*, which provides different angles of the same scene, but how often the camera is actually moving—not much. When it does move, such as when following a character through a set, the movement is smooth and measured.

As much as possible, limit your camera's movement. You want action that emotionally affects the viewer, which is more likely to happen when the camera is stationary and focused on the contents of a scene. A shot that's bouncing, zooming, or otherwise sloshing about like a drunk at happy hour is a scene where the movement is distracting from the action. Of course, there are times when motion is called for: can you imagine reality-television shows like *COPS* or *The Amazing Race* using stationary cameras? I imagine it's difficult enough to chase a suspected criminal down a dark alley and over a chain-link fence without asking him to pause for a few minutes while the crew sets up its lights and tripods.

Staying still has another practical benefit: excess movement causes blurring in your images (**Figure 3.1**). Our eyes do a good job of pulling detail out of motion blur, but there's a limit to how often they can tolerate fuzzy swabs of color streaking across the screen.

✔ Tips

- iMovie's image stabilization feature can help fix camera shake. See Chapter 10.

- To move the camera and keep it steady, consider building your own Steadicam-like rig. See Dan Selakovich's book *Killer Camera Rigs that You Can Build* (www.dvcamerarigs.com).

Figure 3.1 Sudden camera moves introduce blurriness to your footage. Try to keep the camera stationary for most of your shots, if possible.

But If You Must Move...

Okay, you don't have to remain completely still when shooting. In fact, motion can be particularly effective—in moderation. A little motion can go a long way.

Case in point: film director Steven Soderberg. If you watch one of his movies, you'll notice that the camera is almost always in motion, but just barely. A scene in *Ocean's Eleven* stands out in my mind, where a group of main characters steals a device from a research university. In the shot, you're looking down the side of their getaway van toward a set of doors where the crooks will emerge with the device.

It would have been simple to lock the camera down in a fixed location and shoot the actors coming out of the doors. Instead, Soderberg *very slowly* pushes in on a dolly (see "Dollying," later in this chapter). The camera only moves perhaps one or two feet, but the subtle motion draws your attention to the door in a way that a motionless shot would not.

Figure 3.2 Optical zoom and automatic focus can be a great combination when you're shooting something from far away.

Start with the camera zoomed out...

...and slowly zoom in...

...then hold on the zoomed-in image before slowly zooming back out.

Figure 3.3 Quick zooms in and out are effective ways to instill headaches in your viewers. Instead, slowly zoom in, hold, then slowly zoom out. This technique gives you good, clear footage at several distances.

Zooming

Now that I've lectured on the evils of moving your camera, let's get into the realities of the types of motion you'll encounter. To start, let's look at one of the most common trouble-makers, the zoom control.

When you bought your camera, the first thing you probably did was play with the zoom control. It's usually a rocker switch that moves between W (wide) and T (telephoto), and enables you to view distant objects. Combined with a camera's automatic focus feature, especially when shooting in the field, zooming can get you closer to your subject (**Figure 3.2**).

However, the control can be sensitive, leading to abrupt or too-quick zooms in and out. A better approach is to smoothly zoom in on your subject, hold for a bit, then slowly zoom out (**Figure 3.3**). Practice with the control to get a feel for how much pressure is needed, and try to run through the shot a few times before you actually record it.

✔ Tips

- If you missed the memo in Chapter 1: Turn off the digital zoom feature of your camera. The camera tries to enlarge the pixels, thereby appearing to zoom beyond its optical limit. All you really end up with is large blocky pixels.

- Sometimes you want an abrupt zoom, either because it enhances the action or because you don't have time to shoot, stop recording, zoom in, then begin recording again. In the latter case, zoom quickly and hold onto the shot—you can edit out the actual zoom later in iMovie.

- A good zoom can be handy when you're not recording. If you're not toting a pair of binoculars, your camcorder will help you see objects in the distance.

Dollying

Dollying is similar to zooming, in that the camera moves in toward (or away from) a subject. However, a dolly shot doesn't use the zoom control at all. In feature film shoots, a dolly is a platform that holds the camera and rides on rails similar to railroad tracks. When filming, one or more people (known as grips) push the dolly, resulting in a smooth shot.

When you zoom, the camcorder's lens is simulating the appearance of moving closer to your subject. When dollying, you're moving the camera physically closer. The difference is especially pronounced in the background (**Figure 3.4**).

✔ Tips

- As with zooming, you want to ease in and out of a dolly shot. Grips aren't just people who push equipment around. A good grip can accelerate and decelerate smoothly and, often more importantly, *consistently* during multiple takes.

- A dolly shot is a professional-looking camera move, but it's likely you don't have a dolly setup or want to spend the money to rent one. Instead, choose from a number of alternative dollies. Wheelchairs are great (and comfortable for filming!), and skateboards also work in a pinch. It doesn't matter so much *how* you get the shot, only that the shot turns out the way you want it.

Zoomed in

Pushed in on dolly, no zoom

Figure 3.4 These two shots are similarly framed, but look at the orange building in the background to see how the two approaches differ.

Automatic

1/2000 shutter speed

Figure 3.5 Higher shutter speeds can make fast-moving objects appear clearer.

Changing Shutter Speed

Your camcorder doesn't have a shutter in the traditional sense. There's no little door that opens and closes quickly to control the amount of light that gets through the lens. However, camcorders can simulate shutter speed by controlling how quickly the CCD sensors refresh the image being recorded, which is measured in times per second. A normal shutter speed is approximately 1/60th of a second, meaning the CCD samples an image 60 times per second.

Why change shutter speed? Using a higher setting is good for capturing fast-moving action like sporting events. The blur caused by moving objects is substantially reduced at speeds of 1/4000 or 1/8000, creating frames that contain very little blurring (**Figure 3.5**). You'll need to experiment with your camera's settings, though; a high shutter speed can also make the image appear to strobe, or flash artificially.

✔ Tips

- Faster shutter speeds require more light. If you think of a traditional shutter, not as much light enters the camera when the shutter is closing more times per second. So a dimly lit room can appear even darker at a high shutter speed.

- Your camcorder is probably changing shutter speeds without your knowledge. On Auto setting, it detects what kind of light is present, and if it detects fluorescent lighting—which flickers imperceptibly to our eyes, but can cause havoc on a digital recording—the shutter speed automatically changes to compensate.

Panning

Want to capture the grandeur of a landscape or show more of a scene than will fit in the camera's frame? You can pivot the camera left or right and not disrupt the scene with too much motion. This side-to-side movement is called panning. A similar shot, tilting, moves the camera up and down, though it's not used as frequently.

To pan a scene:

1. Mount your camera on a tripod for best results, or hold it as steady as you can.

2. Determine where the pan will begin and end.

3. Begin recording at the first point, and pivot the camera left or right at an even pace. If your camera is not on a tripod, swivel your body steadily at the hips.

4. When you reach the end point of your pan, stop recording.

Pan ahead of subjects

A panning shot often follows a subject from one side of the screen to the other, but think of your composition as you do this. Don't just center the subject in the frame. Instead, provide space into which the person can walk by panning ahead of him (**Figure 3.6**).

✔ Tips

- To help stabilize the camera while you're holding it, pull your elbows in close to your body, hold the camera with both hands, and keep a wide stance.

- As it turns out, the biggest problem with panning isn't moving the camera smoothly. Your top concern should be: Is the horizon level? If the camera isn't exactly even with the horizon, panning will give the effect of moving uphill or downhill (**Figure 3.7**).

Figure 3.6 Frame your shots when panning so that subjects walk into the shot, not out the edges.

Figure 3.7 It's either you or the camera—the world just doesn't naturally tip like that.

- If you're using a tripod, be sure to get a fluid-head tripod. It's more expensive than your standard unit, but allows for much smoother motion.

- Panning doesn't have to involve rotating the camera around a central axis. Use a dolly setup (see "Dollying," earlier) to move the camera from side to side.

LIGHTING

Unless you plan to shoot with the lens cap on, you'll have to come to grips with lighting in your videos. Put simply, you want to have enough light to see what's being filmed, but not so much that it blows out the camcorder's sensors with pure white. You also don't want scenes that are so dark you can't see what's going on.

When a Hollywood film crew shoots a movie, the lighting you see is enhanced (or outright artificial—even the most natural-looking sunlight coming through a window is likely a big spotlight on the other side of the wall). You don't need to go to those extremes, of course. Most often your lighting rigs will entail the sun, some lamps, and maybe a spotlight or two.

What's important is that you know how basic lighting works, and how to take advantage of it to ensure that the objects you're shooting don't turn out to be dark, talking blobs when you're editing.

Hard and Soft Light

There are infinite possible combinations of light, which can seem daunting when you're shooting video. Fortunately, for our purposes we can break light into two broad categories: hard and soft.

Figure 4.1 Hard light creates sharp, clearly defined shadows. A bright halogen lamp is providing the light.

◆ **Hard light.** The term hard light refers to the light produced by a direct source, which creates shadows with clearly defined edges (**Figure 4.1**). Hard light tends to be bright, like the sun at midday.

◆ **Soft light.** In contrast, soft light isn't as direct, and produces shadows that are blurred at the edges or fade away (**Figure 4.2**). Soft light is typically light filtered by artificial means (such as hoods and filters attached to the light) or by natural means (such as clouds, fog, or shade).

In general, soft light is better to film by, because it gives you more levels of brightness and accentuates natural textures. Hard light creates a lot of contrast, limiting the brightness levels because you see either high-intensity light or deep, dark shadows.

Figure 4.2 Soft light diffuses the shadows, making them blurry or even fade out gradually. In this case, a white t-shirt was put in front of the halogen bulb to dampen its intensity. (Hey, we're real high-tech at the Carlson world headquarters.)

✔ Tip

■ If lighting is particularly important to a scene, add a video monitor to your list of equipment to bring on a video shoot. Although your camcorder offers a viewfinder and an LCD, you won't know how the image will look on a TV screen until you see it projected on a monitor. The camera's LCD is great for viewing the content you're capturing, but LCDs can often display images brighter than they're being recorded; or, if you're outside, the LCD's pixels can get washed out by the sunlight.

White balance, indoors

White balance, outdoors

Figure 4.3 Many camcorders feature the capability to adjust the color temperature they display.

Color Temperature

White light is a combination of all the colors of the spectrum, as you've seen when playing with a prism or looking at a rainbow. As such, it's not going to always be white while you're filming—a myriad of factors can make images appear with a colored cast, leading to video footage that looks a little too green, or blue, or any number of shifts.

Your camcorder automatically adjusts to compensate for this *color temperature* of the light by setting the white balance. Essentially, this is the color that the camera sees as white, causing the camera to adjust the display of the rest of the colors based on this setting. You probably have a few basic controls for changing the setting, such as Auto, Indoor, or Outdoor presets (**Figure 4.3**).

You may also be able to specify the white point manually by selecting Manual and filming a sheet of white paper in the environment where you'll be shooting; the camera uses the values it captured as the basis for displaying the other colors.

✔ Tip

■ It's best to get the color temperature right when you're shooting, but you can compensate for color casts in iMovie using the Video Adjustments controls. See Chapter 10 for more information.

Three-Point Lighting

If you have more control over the way your scene is lit, try to use a basic three-point lighting setup. This allows for plenty of light to illuminate the scene, while also reducing deep shadows. A three-point setup consists of a *key light*, a *fill light*, and a *back light* (**Figure 4.4**).

The key light is the primary light source in your scene, and usually the brightest. The fill light is softer, filling in the shadows and adding texture, and is often dimmer than the key light to avoid washing out the image and flattening it. The back light is often small, focused, and used to help separate the scene's subject from the background.

As an easy example, let's say you're setting up to shoot an interview (**Figure 4.5**). Remember, this is just a basic configuration—you can position the lights any way you choose.

To set up three-point lighting:

1. With the camera facing the interview subject, position the key light to the right and slightly forward of the camera. Raise the light so that it's at a 35- to 45-degree angle, pointing down at the subject.

2. Position the fill light to the left of the camera and subject, approximately halfway between the two. The fill prevents deep shadows caused by the key.

3. Place the back light behind the subject, raised a bit higher than the key light, and aimed so that it illuminates the back of the subject's head and shoulders.

Fill light   Back light   Key light

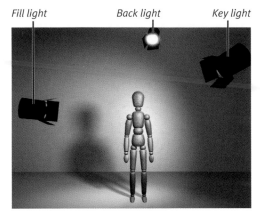

Figure 4.4 A basic lighting setup involves three lights, though of course you can use more (or less).

Key light only

Key light and fill light

Key, fill, and back lights

Figure 4.5 You could use just a key light, a fill and key, or any other combination of lights. Shown here is the progression of adding lights.

Figure 4.6 A strong light source behind your subjects can easily make them appear as silhouettes.

✔ Tips

- Your camcorder is programmed to automatically adjust the exposure (the amount of light coming in). You've probably seen this happen when you move from a bright area to a dark one, as details come into view after a second or two. To minimize this extreme change of contrast, break up your shots so the camera can make the adjustment when you're not filming.

- You've seen the silhouettes. When the key light is behind your subject—whether it's the sun, an especially bright white wall, or a lamp in the background—the camera picks up on the light area in favor of the dark, and pretty soon the person in your video looks like a mob informant protecting his identity (**Figure 4.6**). Try to shoot with the light coming from behind you or from one side, so the light falls on the person or object you're filming.

- When a back light spills directly into the frame, you get the visual artifact known as lens flare. Repositioning your light usually fixes the problem.

- Keep in mind that you don't need to raid a professional camera store and stock up on lighting equipment. You probably have all the lights you need at home or in your office, if you're willing to move things around a bit. Just be careful not to shed too much light onto a scene, which will make it appear flat and less interesting.

- Three-point lighting is a good minimum starting point. On some productions, dozens of light sources may be used to light a scene properly.

THREE-POINT LIGHTING

Bounce Cards and Reflectors

You don't need a truckload of lights to illuminate your scene. A common and easy solution for shedding more light on your subject is to use a bounce card or reflector. These are either pieces of cardboard, cloth, or wood that are colored white, gray, or silver to reflect light into shadowy areas. You can buy inexpensive flexible reflectors that twist into a compact circle for storage. You could also create your own reflectors—white poster board covered with aluminum foil on one side, for example.

Have someone hold the reflector, or mount it on something, and aim its reflection as you would with a fill light.

✔ Tips

- Bounce light onto a person's face, but don't bounce it into their eyes. Yeah, it's a mean thing to do, but more importantly (for our purposes, anyway), it makes him squint, hiding the eyes, which are often a subject's most compelling feature.

- iMovie includes the capability to adjust brightness and contrast in a movie clip, but it won't fix a poorly lit scene. In fact, cranking up the brightness often washes out the image, because the setting is applied evenly throughout the frame. See Chapter 10 to learn how to apply video adjustments in iMovie.

Figure 4.7 Shooting in the middle of the day can create sharp shadows.

Shooting Outside

It's one thing to configure lighting in a dark room where you have absolute control. But the rules become much more slippery when you're filming outside, where the sun and clouds can change the lighting from moment to moment. No matter where you're filming, you can make choices that take advantage of the weather.

◆ Avoid shooting in the middle of the day when the sun is directly overhead. A key light from above casts shadows down across the face, which obscures a person's eyes and can give the appearance of a hung-over Frankenstein (**Figure 4.7**).

◆ Clouds are your friends. A good layer of cloud cover is an excellent diffuser of sunlight, providing a more even level of light in your scene. Coupled with a few well-placed bounce cards and a fill light, a typical cloudy day can provide warmer tones than you might expect.

◆ Shade is also your friend. Again, you want to minimize high-contrast key lighting and enhance the balance between shadows and fill light. Move to the shade of a tree (which can also provide its own unique shadow textures, depending on the tree) or to the side of a building.

◆ To maximize natural light, shoot early or late in the day, when the sun is near the horizon. The light isn't as harsh, you can get some very intriguing shadows, and the color of the scene is generally warmer and more inviting.

✔ Tip

■ If you must shoot in the middle of a sunny day, put some light-colored fabric above your subject to act as a diffuser.

CAPTURING AUDIO

Video gets all the attention. When new camcorders are released, companies hype the image resolution, the color fidelity, the zoom ratios, optics...oh, and there's a microphone in there somewhere, too.

Well, you'll discover soon enough how important audio is. You can spend hours setting up your lighting and composition, but if the sound is poor, your scene is poor. The good news is, for most casual shooters, the built-in mic will capture what you're filming. Some cameras include controls for varying input levels, while most others offer automatic gain control (AGC) to manage the input without your involvement. However, even if you're going to be filming informally, consider purchasing a separate microphone.

As with lighting, you can spend your life learning the complexities of audio production. This chapter is intended as an overview of some options available for capturing audio.

Headphones

If sound is at all important to you, pack a pair of headphones when you go shooting (**Figure 5.1**). You can use almost any old pair (earbud-style headphones, for example, are extremely portable), but what's important is that you can hear what your camcorder is recording.

When you're standing behind the camera, your ears are naturally picking out the audio in the scene and ignoring other ambient noises. Your camera's microphone isn't nearly as sophisticated, and does its best to maintain a level input based on all the noise in the immediate vicinity. Camcorder mics can also be sensitive to movement, picking up the sound of you shifting the camera or adjusting the focus.

A pair of headphones screens out the noise around you and gives you a direct bead on what the camera is hearing. And, it's the best audio troubleshooting device on the market: if you can't hear your subject, you'll know right away, instead of later on when you're editing in iMovie.

Figure 5.1 Wearing headphones while shooting is the only accurate way to know what your camera is recording.

Built-in microphone

Figure 5.2 The camera's built-in microphone is good, but it's susceptible to picking up noise from the camera and doesn't record distant subjects too well.

Your Camcorder's Microphone

I don't want to give the impression that a camcorder's built-in microphone is a flimsy afterthought. On the contrary, it's a sophisticated device that does the best it can, given the circumstances. Where it falls flat at times is with its placement: Because camcorders are so small, there isn't much room for a microphone (**Figure 5.2**), so you're bound to pick up sounds that the camera is making (such as the motor advancing the tape, or the zoom control adjusting the lens).

Another limitation is distance. The most important factor when recording audio is the distance between the microphone and subject—the closer the better. If you're filming a birthday party, for example, you're likely to be right in the action and will pick up audio pretty well. But what about when you're doing an interview? You want the person's comments to be picked up clearly, but you don't want the camcorder to be in her face. If you're shooting from a moderate distance (see "Depth of Field" in Chapter 2), the microphone won't pick up the sound clearly.

✔ Tip

- Camera manufacturers are starting to realize that audio recording can be a compelling selling point. A few camcorders record in Dolby 5.1 stereo surround sound.

12-bit versus 16-bit audio

Some camcorders include the option to record in 12-bit or 16-bit audio. When you're recording in 12-bit, the microphone is grabbing sound in stereo and saving it to two separate channels (left and right), leaving two more channels to record more audio in the camera later. If you choose to record in 16-bit audio, the quality is a bit better than what you'd hear from a CD—you're sampling more audio data than in 12-bit mode.

Now, with the definitions out of the way, *forget about 12-bit audio*. Although 16-bit takes up more disk space, iMovie prefers it; 12-bit has been known to cause audio dropouts and other problems. Plus, iMovie ignores 12-bit's two separate stereo tracks anyway, so from the software's perspective, it's just one audio stream.

Wind Screen mode

Here's a good general tip: read your camcorder manual before you go on vacation. If I hadn't been in such a hurry to take a break, I would have discovered the Wind Screen feature of my camcorder, which does a decent job of cutting down the extra noise produced by wind blowing into the microphone. It's not a perfect solution (what is?), but it would have made some of my footage sound less like I was in the middle of a tornado.

Ambient Sound

Your biggest concern is likely to be capturing the audio of your main subject, but don't forget about ambient noise. The sounds that surround you can be just as important as the main audio to establish mood or place. It's also good for maintaining *consistent* noise. For example, I took some footage on the airplane en route to my aforementioned vacation, but when I brought it into iMovie, the engine noise differed depending on when the video was shot (when we started to descend) and even what side of the plane I was filming. However, I was able to use a sample of ambient noise in the background to provide an even level of noise (and also to adjust the audio so it wasn't as dominant). Record ambient noise whenever possible—you can spend a few minutes before or after your primary shooting and get plenty of material to work with later in iMovie.

This tip applies to "quiet" rooms as well. Even an empty room has its own audio signature—it's never completely silent. Grab a minute or two of quiet noise, too.

Figure 5.3 A simple clip-on lavalier microphone can greatly increase the quality of your recorded audio.

Directional microphone

Figure 5.4 Higher-end digital camcorders are outfitted with directional microphones that aren't as likely to pick up camera (or camera operator) noise.

Microphones

Remember earlier I said you could spend years mastering the art of capturing audio? As with any specialized field, you could also spend a fortune on microphones and audio equipment. The good news is that you can also spend around $20 at Radio Shack and get what you need. Since you're unlikely to spend tens of thousands of dollars on microphones to use with a $500 camcorder, I'm going to stick with a few realistic options.

Lavalier

A simple and portable solution is to purchase a lavalier microphone (**Figure 5.3**). It clips to your subject's shirt or tie, and often has a small battery-powered amplifier, making it a condenser mic, which is how your camcorder's documentation refers to it.

Directional

Directional microphones come in a number of shapes and sizes, and are built to pick up sound in some areas and not others. For example, cardioid microphones minimize sound coming from the sides and block sound from behind.

A shotgun mic, like the ones found on higher-end camcorders (**Figure 5.4**), picks up audio only in front of the camera (or whatever the mic is pointed at) while ignoring sound from behind the mic (reducing the likelihood of recording camera noise).

An omnidirectional microphone, on the other hand, picks up sound from all sides and is good to use when you're not focused on any one particular subject.

✔ Tip

■ Companies like Røde (www.rodemic.com) now offer affordable directional mics designed for consumer cameras.

Wireless

Wireless microphones also come in a variety of shapes and sizes, but aren't tied to an audio cable that snakes back to the camcorder. They're portable, allowing you more freedom to shoot your video while moving, or from anywhere in the room. The biggest drawback to using a wireless mic is that it's more likely to pick up interference from other radio sources, so be sure to test the output before you start filming, and use headphones to monitor the recording while shooting.

✔ Tips

■ Check your camcorder's specifications for attaching external microphones. Some require that the mic is amplified, calling for an external power source. Other cameras can use the camcorder's battery to provide power.

■ If you don't entirely trust your camcorder's mic, or just want to be sure you have a backup source of audio, consider purchasing a MiniDisc recorder so you can make an additional recording of a scene's audio while you're filming. It stores audio digitally, which you can import into iMovie and add to your movie, or use in place of audio that didn't record clearly (due to the placement of the microphone, for example). Another option, if your audio doesn't need to be at high quality, is to use a Belkin voice recorder (www.belkin.com) attached to an iPod.

■ If you're dubbing dialogue, you may have to break the audio into several clips in iMovie and synchronize the timing often, but that's a better solution than trying to re-create the original shoot. See Chapter 12 for more on editing audio.

Part 2
Editing in
iMovie

Make a
Movie in a Hurry

6

The whole point of iMovie '09 is to make editing your video faster and easier. So in that spirit, this chapter offers a stripped-down walkthrough of the video editing experience.

In subsequent chapters I cover each step in more detail, but if you're burning to turn your footage into a movie and share it with the world, this is the place to start. Keep in mind that iMovie offers several ways to perform some tasks; for example, I've shown only two ways to trim a clip here, but more methods are described in Chapter 10.

Enough of this rambling already. Let's edit!

Make a Movie in a Hurry

Make a Movie in a Hurry

For this overview, we're going to import video from a digital camcorder, assemble a short movie from the footage, edit the video, add transitions, titles, and a soundtrack, upload it to YouTube.com for others to view, and then finally burn a copy on DVD. More information can be found in the chapters referenced in parentheses.

To create a new project (*Chapter 7*):

1. Choose New Project from the File menu.

2. Enter a name for the movie you're about to create and choose an aspect ratio that matches the video you shot (**Figure 6.1**).

3. This dialog also lets you apply a theme to the project, but for our purposes here, keep the theme set to None. Click Create.

To import footage (*Chapter 8*):

1. Connect the camcorder to your Mac using FireWire or USB cables, depending on the camera.

2. Switch the camera to Play or VCR mode and launch iMovie. The import window should appear.

3. Set the mode switch at the left side of the window to Automatic and press the Import button.

4. In the dialog that appears, enter a name for the new Event where the video will be stored and then click Import (**Figure 6.2**). For this example, disable the option to analyze the clips for stabilization so you don't have to wait to start editing. All footage on tape or memory (depending on model) is imported.

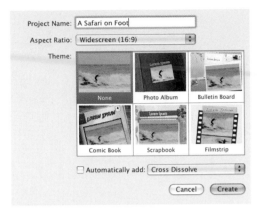

Figure 6.1 Give your new project a name, specify its aspect ratio, and optionally choose a theme.

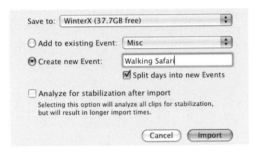

Figure 6.2 Every batch of imported video is saved as an Event in iMovie's Event Library.

Figure 6.3 Drag to select the video footage you want to include in your movie.

Add Selection to Project button

Figure 6.4 Drag the selected clip to the Project Browser to add it to your movie.

Figure 6.5 Congratulations, you've created a rough cut of your movie!

Figure 6.6 Choose Clip Trimmer from the Action pop-up menu.

To assemble your movie (*Chapters 9 and 10*):

1. In the Event Browser at the bottom of the screen, move your mouse pointer over the video thumbnails to preview the footage; to play a clip in real time, position the mouse pointer over a clip and press the spacebar.

2. Choose a clip you want to add to your movie and click its thumbnail to select a four-second portion of a clip; drag the left or right edge to adjust the selection (**Figure 6.3**).

3. Click and hold in the middle of the selection and then drag it to the Project Browser (**Figure 6.4**).

   (You can also click the Add Selection to Project button, or simply press the E key.) The clip is now part of your movie.

4. Continue adding clips to the Project Browser; in no time you'll have a rough cut of your movie (**Figure 6.5**).

   Position the mouse pointer on a clip and press the space bar to play the video in the Viewer; you can also press the \ (backslash) key to play your movie from the beginning.

5. If you want to rearrange the order of the clips, select one and drag it to a new location. Dropping it onto an existing clip splits that clip at the point where you released the mouse button.

To edit clips (*Chapter 10*):

1. Trim the length of a clip by choosing Clip Trimmer from the Action pop-up menu (**Figure 6.6**). The Clip Trimmer appears over the Event browser area.

continues on next page

2. Drag the left or right edge of the clip to change its duration.

   Footage that appears within the yellow box is visible in your movie. Other footage (dimmed) is hidden; you can always get it back later if needed (**Figure 6.7**). Click Done to apply the edit.

   For more refined edits, double-click the space between two clips to edit the *cut point* in the Precision Editor. The clip before the edit appears on top; the clip after appears below.

   Drag each clip left or right to set where the cut point is (**Figure 6.8**).

3. Continue editing clips until you're happy with the length of the movie.

To add a photo from iPhoto (*Chapter 11*):

1. Click the Photos button (or press Command-2) to view a list of photo sources on your computer (**Figure 6.9**).

2. Choose a photo below the Photos list and drag it to the Project Browser (**Figure 6.10**). Dragging an Event adds all images from that event. The Ken Burns Effect is applied by default; you can edit it later if you choose.

To add a transition (*Chapter 13*):

1. Click the Transitions button (or press Command-4) to display thumbnails of the available transitions.

2. Drag a thumbail from the Transitions Browser to the Project Browser; a solid green bar between clips indicates where the transition will appear when you release the mouse button (**Figure 6.11**).

Figure 6.7 The Clip Trimmer shows all of the clip's footage, even if you didn't add it all to the movie.

Figure 6.8 Dragging the bottom clip changes the first frame that appears after the cut point (the blue line).

Photos button

Figure 6.9 iMovie can use photos from other Apple programs such as iPhoto and Aperture.

Figure 6.10 Drag a photo from the Photos Browser to your movie to create a picture with the Ken Burns Effect applied.

Make a Movie in a Hurry

Cross Dissolve transition

Figure 6.11 Drag a transition to the position between two clips. Each transition type has its own icon so you can easily tell what has been applied.

Apply a title   Title added

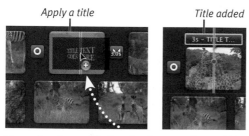

Figure 6.12 Drag a title thumbnail onto a clip to add it. The title appears as an icon above the video.

Figure 6.13 Type the title text directly into the Viewer.

Figure 6.14 The green background tells you the song will be an underlying soundtrack.

To add a title (*Chapter 13*):

1. Click the Titles button (or press Command-3) to view the Titles Browser.

2. Drag a title thumbnail to the location in your movie where you want the title to appear (**Figure 6.12**).

   To make the title overlay the video, drag it directly on top of the clip (you can easily reposition it if you don't hit the precise location at first). Dragging a title to an empty space between clips creates the title on a black background.

   After you release the mouse button, the title appears as a blue icon above the video.

3. With the title still selected, enter the title's text in the Viewer (**Figure 6.13**). Click Done to apply the title.

To add a soundtrack (*Chapter 12*):

1. Click the Music and Sound Effects button (or press Command-1) to view a list of audio sources that iMovie recognizes.

2. Preview a song by selecting it and clicking the Play button, or double-clicking the title.

3. When you've chosen one to use, drag it to the Project Browser and release it when the background turns green (**Figure 6.14**).

   This method sets the song as a background soundtrack; dropping the song onto a video clip adds the song to that position in the movie (for simplicity, I'm sticking with a soundtrack in this example).

To share your movie to YouTube (*Chapter 16*):

1. When you're ready to make your movie public, choose YouTube from the Share menu. (YouTube isn't the only sharing method, of course, but it's one of the easiest for our example.)

2. In the YouTube dialog that appears, you may need to specify (or set up) your YouTube account. Click the Add button and follow the instructions; you'll need to do this only once.

3. Choose a category and enter a title, description, and any tags (which make it easier for people to find the movie) (**Figure 6.15**).

4. Choose a size for the final movie, Mobile or Medium, depending on how you expect people to watch the movie.

5. To share the movie only with people you choose, mark the checkbox labeled Make this movie personal.

6. Click Next, read the YouTube Terms of Service, and then click Publish to encode and upload your movie to the Web.

7. After several minutes (depending on the movie's length and the published size), iMovie gives you the Web address and an option to send it to a friend.

✔ Tips

- If you want to create a DVD containing your movie, see Chapters 18, 19, and 20.

- To watch the movie I created in this chapter, point your Web browser to http://www.youtube.com/watch?v=7MYqEGEf7aM

Figure 6.15 Uploading your movie directly to YouTube enables many people to view the movie.

Make a Movie in a Hurry

iMovie Overview

Getting iMovie '09

If you bought a Mac after February 2009, iMovie '09 should already be installed. Otherwise, you need to purchase iLife '09, Apple's $79 suite of digital hub applications (www.apple.com/ilife/), which includes iMovie, iDVD, iPhoto, GarageBand, and iWeb.

If iMovie '08 is already installed, the iLife '09 installer will overwrite it. If you want to keep a copy just in case, rename the "iMovie" application to "iMovie '08" before installing iLife '09.

If you still have a copy of iMovie HD 6, the iLife installer ignores it, and you can still use it. Unfortunately, iMovie HD 6 is no longer available as a free download, which was the case when iMovie '08 was released.

iMovie runs only under Mac OS X 10.5.6 or later and only on a Mac containing an Intel processor, a Power Mac G5 (dual 2.0 GHz or faster), or an iMac G5 (1.9 GHz or faster).

Being a fan of the moviemaking process, I enjoy reading "behind the scenes" articles about how films are produced. In nearly all cases, the reporter interviews cast and crew at the movie set during shooting (and invariably makes it sound more exciting than it usually is). But filming is only one part of the production.

Rarely reported is the editing stage, when the editor (often with the director) spends long hours in a dark editing room—sometimes for many months—shaping hours of raw footage into what we eventually see in a theater. They grab the best takes from each day's shooting, assemble them according to the storyline, and then add transitions, audio, special effects, and whatever else is required for that particular flick.

The process of making your digital video is similar (minus the reporters and possibly the long hours). By this point you've shot your footage, but that doesn't mean you have a movie. Here's where iMovie and digital non-linear editing can take your mass of video and audio and turn it into a movie. This chapter introduces iMovie, makes sure you have the tools you need to get started, and gives you an overview of the program's unexpectedly powerful yet simple interface.

iMovie's Interface

In iMovie, everything happens in one big window (**Figure 7.1**). Use the resize control in the lower-right corner to change the window's size, or click the green Zoom button in the upper-left corner to maximize the window.

The interface comprises three main areas: the Project Library, where you assemble your movie; the Viewer, where you preview clips; and the Event Library, where you store your footage. A toolbar bisects the window.

✔ Tips

- To help improve performance, try reducing iMovie's window to its minimum size. If the Monitor is smaller, iMovie doesn't need to expend as much processing power drawing video on the screen.

- The actual version number of the program is iMovie 8.0.1 (as of this writing), but Apple calls it either "iMovie" or "iMovie '09." I prefer the latter two, since this iMovie is more accurately a version 2.0 iteration (iMovie '08 was created from scratch). I'll refer to the version number only when needed.

Click to view the Project Library   Project Browser   Viewer

Event list   Event Browser   Toolbar

Figure 7.1 iMovie is comprised of three main sections: the Project Library (1); the Viewer (2); and the Event Library (3). The Project Library and Event Library each break down into a list and an area to browse the footage.

Click to return to the Project Browser.

Figure 7.2 The Project Library contains all your projects, including those on other hard disks.

Play from beginning

View projects or events

Turn Cover Flow view on or off

Auto hide thumbstrip

Figure 7.3 Using the controls at the edges of the screen, view your projects in full-screen mode.

The Project Library

The Project Library is where you find your projects. When you're editing, the Project Library is hidden to make more room for the Project Browser. Click the Project Library button to reveal it (**Figure 7.2**).

To preview a movie:

◆ Click a movie to select it, and then drag the mouse pointer over the preview film-strip to the right of each movie title.

◆ With a project selected, press the spacebar to play from the current location of the playhead. Or, click the Play Project from Beginning (Command-\) button or Play Project Full-Screen button (Command-G).

To view the Project Library full-screen:

◆ Choose Show Projects full-screen from the Window menu (or press Command-6). The currently-selected movie is ready to play, with other projects stacked to the sides in iMovie's Cover Flow interface (**Figure 7.3**). When you move the mouse pointer, additional controls appear:

▲ Press the spacebar or click the Play Project from Beginning button to watch the movie.

▲ Switch between viewing your Project Library and your Event Library.

▲ Turn off Apple's Cover Flow mode if you want to view just the thumbstrip for the active movie.

▲ Hide the thumbstrip while the movie is playing, or make it always visible.

▲ Drag the scrollbar at the bottom to view other movies.

✔ Tip

■ In addition to viewing a movie in the Project Library without actually opening its project, you can share it and even print it (seriously, see Chapter 9).

The Project Library

The Project Browser

The Project Browser is where you assemble and edit a movie. It displays your movie's clips from left to right and top to bottom, the same way you're reading this paragraph (**Figure 7.4**). The major components of the browser include (but are not limited to, as we'll see later):

◆ **Filmstrip.** All video clips appear in the filmstrip as a series of thumbnails. When a clip includes more thumbnails than will fit on a line, iMovie indicates the visual break with a jagged edge. Transitions are indicated by icons between clips, and other elements, such as titles and audio clips, show up above or below the clips.

◆ **Playhead.** Move your mouse pointer to any point on the filmstrip and you'll see the playhead, a red vertical line that indicates which frame is currently showing in the Viewer.

◆ **Soundtrack.** A soundtrack is an audio file (usually a song) that plays behind the video. It's represented by a green field that literally sits behind the filmstrip. (See Chapter 12 for more on editing audio.)

◆ **Clips size slider.** This control determines how many thumbnails each clip displays. A setting of "5s" means iMovie is creating a new thumbnail for every 5 seconds of footage. Drag the slider to choose from "1/2s" (one frame for every half second, showing more images) to All (just one thumbnail for each clip) (**Figure 7.5**).

Filmstrip   Playhead   Clip (selected)   Soundtrack

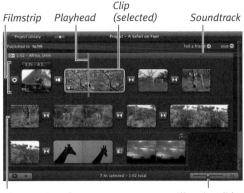

Clip, continued   Clips size slider

Figure 7.4 An edited movie in the Project Browser.

1/2s (half second)

2s (2 seconds)

All

Figure 7.5 Selecting a smaller time setting in the thumbnail control displays more images for each clip.

Playhead

Figure 7.6 The Viewer displays the footage under the playhead and is where you watch movie playback.

Figure 7.7 With the Viewer set to Small, there's more work area for the Event Library (compare this to Figure 7.1, which is set to Medium).

The Viewer

The Viewer is the window to your footage, displaying whatever frame of video appears at the current playhead location. It's also where you watch playback of your movie (**Figure 7.6**).

The Viewer can also be resized in one of three preset configurations; for example, making the Viewer smaller frees more room to browse the Event Library (**Figure 7.7**). From the Window menu, go to Viewer and then choose Small, Medium, or Large (or press Command-8, Command-9, or Command-0, respectively).

Resizing the iMovie window as a whole (by dragging the lower-right corner) also changes the Viewer's size proportionally, as does dragging the toolbar.

✔ Tip

■ If you work with two monitors, iMovie can shift the Viewer to one as a secondary display (**Figure 7.8**). Make sure the Show Advanced Tools option is enabled in iMovie's preferences, and then choose Viewer on Secondary Display from the Window menu.

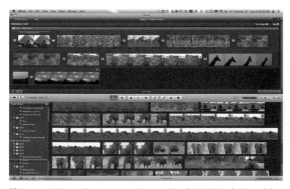

Figure 7.8 My main computer is a 15-inch MacBook Pro with a 20-inch external display connected to expand my screen real estate. The 20-inch screen is set up as my main display (at left), leaving the laptop's built-in screen acting as the secondary display (at right). Moving the Viewer to the secondary display frees a lot of horizontal space in the Project Browser for editing.

The Event Library

The Event Library allows me to find all of my footage in one place. As you'll see in the next chapter, iMovie organizes imported video into Events, listed in reverse chronological order in the Event list (**Figure 7.9**).

Clicking an Event displays its footage in the Event Browser. As with the Project Library, you can control how many thumbnails are visible by dragging the clips size slider located below the browser (**Figure 7.10**).

The Event list can also display more information than what originally appears.

To customize the Event list display:

◆ **Date ranges.** In iMovie's preferences, enable the option titled Show date ranges in Event lists to see the start and end dates of the footage (**Figure 7.11**).

◆ **Events by month.** To break down the timeline further, choose Events by Month from the View menu (**Figure 7.12**).

◆ **Events by day.** Need more granularity? Choose Separate Days in Events from the View menu to have each day's footage broken out into separate rows in the Event Browser.

◆ **Volumes.** iMovie recognizes video stored on other hard drives. Click the View Events by Volume button, or choose Events by Volume from the View menu (**Figure 7.13**).

Figure 7.9 Video is organized by Event and listed in chronological order.

Clips size slider

Figure 7.10 The clips size slider controls how many images appear for the clips in the Event Browser.

Figure 7.11 It can be helpful to see date ranges for Events to know at a glance when the video was shot.

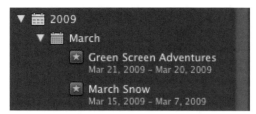

Figure 7.12 Another way to view Events is by grouping them into months.

View Events by Volume button

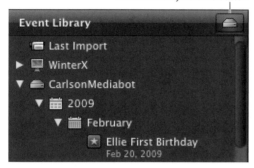

Figure 7.13 iMovie typically stores video on your Mac's internal hard disk, but it can also see other drives.

✔ Tips

■ Events that span two or more months are grouped under the month of the most recent video when the Events by Month option is enabled.

■ Even if you don't have the date ranges option enabled in iMovie's preferences, clicking an Event displays the range at the top of the Event Browser.

■ Click and drag the toolbar up or down to resize the main areas.

■ If a volume isn't currently connected, it won't show up in the Event Library when View Events by Volume is enabled. But when it comes back online, iMovie includes it in the list.

■ Like the Project Library, the Event Library can be viewed full-screen. Choose Show Events Full-Screen from the Window menu, or press Command-7. You can also switch between viewing events and projects by clicking the Show Projects or Events button in full-screen mode (see Figure 7.3 several pages back).

The Event Library

Other View Options

A few other features enable you to further customize the workspace for your editing convenience:

◆ **Swap the Event and Project libraries.** When the time comes to edit your project, you can gain some more working room by moving the Project Library to the area below the toolbar. (This arrangement is also similar to the position of the timeline in earlier versions of iMovie if you prefer that placement.) Click the Swap Events and Projects button, or choose Swap Events and Projects from the Window menu (**Figure 7.14**).

◆ **Change thumbnail size.** Drag the thumbnail size slider to enlarge or reduce the size of the filmstrips in both the Library browser and the Event Browser (**Figure 7.15**).

◆ **Use large font.** Maybe you have such a large, high-resolution display that everything looks small—or maybe your eyes just don't see as well anymore. In either case, you can enlarge the project and event titles by opening iMovie's preferences and choosing Use large font for project and Event lists (**Figure 7.16**).

✔ Tip

■ Hold the Shift key when clicking the Swap Events and Projects button to watch the swapping transition move in slow motion. Why would you want to do this? Why not? (Actually, the slow motion option was built into Mac OS X early on as a way to demonstrate the effect.)

Figure 7.14 When you swap the Event and Project libraries, they shift places using the same stretchy effect used when minimizing items to the Dock.

Thumbnail size slider   *Filmstrip at largest size*

Figure 7.15 The thumbnail size slider controls the appearance of the filmstrips in both browsers.

Figure 7.16 The optional larger font size for the Project and Event lists is a little easier to read.

8

IMPORTING FOOTAGE

Whatever the source of your video—AVCHD, DV, or HDV camcorder; digital still camera with a video recording feature; DVD; an iSight camera; or just movie files on your hard drive—it's easy to bring the footage you shot into iMovie for editing.

iMovie organizes everything in Events, which means you don't need to remember where your iMovie projects and video files are located. All your footage appears in iMovie's Event Browser for use with any project.

Importing Clips

Getting video footage into iMovie is a snap: connect your digital camcorder to your Mac via FireWire or USB, and start importing. Your only practical limitation is space on your hard drive—make sure you have plenty.

To connect via FireWire or USB:

1. Quit iMovie if it's running.

2. Plug the FireWire or USB cable into the Mac and the camcorder.

3. Switch the camcorder to VCR, Play, or PC mode (see the device's documentation).

4. Launch iMovie, which recognizes the attached camera and opens the Import window (**Figure 8.1**).

   If the Import window doesn't appear, click the Camera Import Window button (**Figure 8.2**) or press Command-I.

Image stabilization at import

Each import method in this chapter includes the option to analyze the incoming footage for image stabilization after importing it (**Figure 8.3**). You can skip this step and analyze clips later, but consider doing it now. Analyzing for image stabilization takes a *long* time, anywhere from four to eight times the duration of your footage. So, importing an hour of vacation footage could tie up iMovie all day, depending on the amount of shake in your video and the speed of your Mac. It's the perfect task to run overnight while you're sleeping or away from the computer. When you return, all your clips are stabilized (see Chapter 10 for more).

On the other hand, if you think only a few clips would benefit from stabilization, it may be worth the occasional interruption during editing to perform the analysis on a clip-by-clip basis.

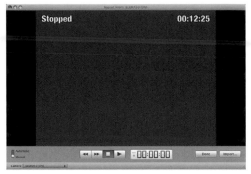

Figure 8.1 Launching iMovie with a camcorder connected automatically opens the Import window.

Figure 8.2 This button opens the Import window.

Figure 8.3 Choose to analyze clips as part of the import process, or skip it until later.

Figure 8.4 iMovie prefers to scale down 1080i video, but you can choose to import it at full size, too.

What If iMovie Won't Read a File Format?

For some reason, iMovie can be finicky about which video formats it chooses to read. Sometimes a file that QuickTime Player opens just fine is rejected by iMovie. What's going on?

The extension you see in a filename—such as .avi or .mpg—doesn't tell the whole story about what kind of file it is. AVI is a container into which the video data is stored. It's the *codec,* the way the video was encoded, that matters.

For example, the movie in **Figure 8.5** was shot using a point-and-shoot still camera. Opening it in QuickTime reveals the codec to be "Microsoft ISO MPEG-4 V1.1".

To make it readable to iMovie, open it in the free MPEG Streamclip (www.squared5.com) and export it as an AIC-formatted QuickTime file. You can also try installing Perian (perian.org) or Flip4Mac (www.telestream.net), two plug-ins that add additional codec support to QuickTime.

| Format: | Microsoft IMA ADPCM, Mono, 44.100 kHz |
| | Microsoft ISO MPEG-4 V1.1, 640 x 480, Millions |

Figure 8.5 The codec revealed in an AVI file.

Choosing an image size for 1080i HD video

Owners of camcorders that shoot high-definition 1080i footage have a choice to make (**Figure 8.4**): import the video at Large (960 x 540) or Full (1920 x 1080) size?

The difference lies as much in iMovie's philosophy of editing as it does with image size. iMovie assumes you're not aiming for the absolute best possible image quality; that instead, you want to edit your home movies quickly and easily. Scaling 1080i HD video to half its resolution enables iMovie to work more efficiently.

Most people will probably not notice a difference. If you're concerned about getting the best HD you can, consider using iMovie HD 6 (if you still have it) or Final Cut Express.

Importing and video formats

In Chapter 1, I talked about camcorder video formats such as DV and AVCHD. Although iMovie can import many different formats, here's where the topic gets more important.

For DV and many MPEG-4 variants, iMovie imports and edits the files natively. High-definition AVCHD and HDV, however, are transcoded to AIC (Apple Intermediate Codec) for better performance while editing.

AVCHD and HDV are highly compressed to fit high-def video onto relatively low-capacity media (memory cards and tape). Instead of storing a full version of every recorded frame, the camcorder saves a complete frame and then updates several successive frames with just the areas of a scene that have changed. During editing, iMovie would need to fill in the rest of those frames on the fly, which slows down everything. Instead the frames are rendered during import and saved to the AIC format.

Importing from a Tapeless Camcorder

Cameras that record video on internal hard drives or memory cards aren't limited to the linearity of tape. The clips are stored wherever there's room on the media like any file on your computer. For that reason, iMovie takes a different importing approach.

To import from a tapeless camcorder:

1. In the Import window, set Automatic or Manual mode. Automatic imports all clips; Manual lets you choose which clips to bring into iMovie.

2. If you chose Automatic, skip to Step 3. If Manual, choose the clips you want to import by marking their checkboxes (**Figure 8.6**). By default, all clips are selected, so you may find it easier to click the Uncheck All button and then choose individual clips.

   To preview a clip, click to select it and press the Play button (**Figure 8.7**).

3. Click the Import All or Import Checked button (depending on the mode).

4. In the dialog that appears (**Figure 8.8**), specify the following:

   ▲ Choose a destination from the Save to pop-up menu. This is likely your computer's internal hard disk, but you can specify any hard disk that's mounted on the Desktop.

   ▲ If the footage is related to an existing Event you've already created, click the radio button marked Add to existing Event and choose the Event from the pop-up menu.

   ▲ Alternately, choose Create new Event and type a name in the field provided (or use the default iMovie gives you).

Figure 8.6 In Manual mode, choose which clips to import from the camcorder.

Play button

Figure 8.7 Click the Play button to review a clip before importing it.

Figure 8.8 Whenever you import footage, you need to create a new Event or assign it to an existing Event.

Figure 8.9 Imported footage appears in the Event Library and the Event Browser.

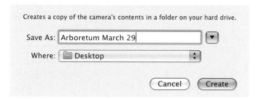

Figure 8.10 Store an unconverted version of your tapeless footage on the hard disk.

Don't Forget to Eject

When you're finished importing, be sure to eject the camcorder's media, which shows up as a mounted volume on your Desktop. Click the Eject button that appears beside the Camera pop-up menu (**Figure 8.11**).

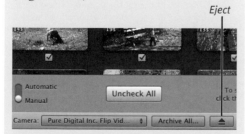

Figure 8.11 Don't forget to eject your tapeless camcorder before unplugging it.

▲ If the footage spans multiple days and you want to organize them separately in the Event Browser, enable Split days into new Events. Otherwise, deselect the checkbox.

▲ If you want iMovie to apply image stabilization to the clips, enable the option marked Analyze for stabilization after import. (But remember, it will take a long time to complete.)

5. For high-definition AVCHD video, choose a size for the imported footage.

6. Click Done to exit the Import window. iMovie imports the footage and transcodes it to AIC for editing. The Event and its footage appear in the Event Library (**Figure 8.9**).

Archiving clips to import later

You may not always have the time to import and transcode your footage—your memory cards or camcorder's hard drive may be full, and there's more to shoot after lunch—but you can still offload those clips to the computer. iMovie's Archive feature copies the contents of your camera's media in its native format to a hard disk, which is much faster than importing. This capability also lets you keep the original footage for storage.

To archive footage:

1. In the Import window, click the Archive All button.

2. Choose a destination and click Create (**Figure 8.10**).

To import archived footage:

1. From the File menu, choose Import > Camera Archive.

2. Locate an archive folder and click Import. iMovie starts the import process described on the opposite page.

Importing from a DV or HDV Camcorder

When you connect a tape-based camcorder, iMovie controls playback and import.

To import all footage from a DV tape:

1. In the Import window, set the mode switch to Automatic (**Figure 8.12**).

2. Click the Import button.

3. In the dialog that appears, create a new Event or choose an existing one (**Figure 8.13**). See Step 4 on the previous pages for details.

4. Click Import. iMovie rewinds the tape, imports all of the footage, and then rewinds the tape again when it's done.

5. Click Done to exit the Import window. The Event and its footage appear in the Event Library.

To import clips from a DV tape:

1. Use the Import window's Playback controls to rewind or forward the camcorder's tape to the spot where you want to begin (**Figure 8.14**).

   To review the video at high speed, click and hold the Rewind or Fast-Forward button (**Figure 8.15**).

2. Click the Import button and specify an Event (see Step 3 on the previous page).

3. Click the Stop button to stop importing.

4. Click Done to exit the Import window.

Figure 8.12 The Automatic mode imports a tape's worth of video without much work on your part.

Figure 8.13 Create an Event and choose to stabilize the footage immediately after import.

Figure 8.14 Use the playback controls to locate the footage you want to import.

Figure 8.15 Click and hold the Rewind or Fast-Forward button while playing to review video at high speed.

Figure 8.16 iMovie indicates the speed at which the video is being captured.

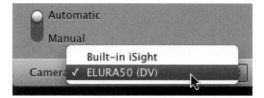

Figure 8.17 Choose a video source.

Importing HDV footage

Importing high-definition video works the same as importing DV, with a couple of differences. iMovie transcodes the HDV footage into AIC, so importing does not happen in real time on many machines. This causes a lag between what you see on the camera's screen and in iMovie—the incoming video is stored in a buffer and then transcoded. The import speed is indicated below iMovie's Monitor (**Figure 8.16**).

For this reason, if you're capturing specific clips (versus an entire tape) don't use iMovie's playback controls to stop importing unless you're capturing in real time—you won't get the footage you expect. Instead, use the camera's LCD screen as a guide and press the camera's Stop button when you reach the end of the footage you want to capture. iMovie then transcodes the rest of the footage in its buffer.

✔ Tips

- iMovie supports having more than one video source attached to your Mac. Click the Camera button and select a camcorder from the pop-up menu (**Figure 8.17**).

- Pressing the Esc key also closes the Import window.

- Audio does not play back during import.

- When you click the Import button, iMovie calculates how much video can be saved to your hard drive and displays the amount in the Save to pop-up menu.

- HDV camcorders can also record DV footage, so make sure the camera is set to the right format before you import.

- If you want to import your video to an external FireWire hard drive, get one with a speed of at least 7,200 RPM.

What Happened to Magic iMovie?

The Magic iMovie feature introduced in iMovie HD is gone in iMovie '09, but some of its capabilities remain. The Automatic import mode rewinds your tape and brings in all clips. You can also automatically add a transition between each clip in the Project Properties dialog (see Chapter 13).

Importing live video

Some cameras can record directly to iMovie.

To import live video:

1. Connect the camera to your Mac, and ensure that it has no tape inserted. If you're using Apple's iSight camera (built into many models), you can skip Step 3.

2. Launch iMovie.

3. Switch the camcorder to Camera or Record mode.

4. Bring up the Import window if it doesn't appear automatically (**Figure 8.18**).

5. Click the Import button; you don't need to use the camera's Record button. For an iSight, the button is labeled Capture.

6. In the Event dialog, choose an existing Event or create a new one. Click Capture.

7. Click the Stop button to end recording.

8. Click Done to exit the Import window.

Figure 8.18 Capture live video (like this gem) using an iSight camera or a camcorder set to Record mode.

The Biggest Hard Drive Isn't Large Enough

When you begin working with digital video, your concept of disk space changes forever. For example, one second of DV footage equals 3.6 MB on disk, which translates roughly to 13 GB of space per hour of video. One hour of high-definition footage occupies anywhere between 38 GB to 50 GB of space.

Fortunately, hard drives are cheaper every day: a quick search for a 1 TB (terabyte) internal drive turns up prices between $100 and $120 as of this writing (try www.dealmac.com).

RAID Storage

Most likely, buying one or two external hard drives will provide the storage you need. However, if you find yourself doing a lot of iMovie editing, consider buying or assembling a RAID (redundant array of inexpensive disks). By making two or more hard drives work in tandem, you can view their combined storage capacity as one volume, and potentially speed up performance.

A hardware RAID system, such as the Drobo (www.drobo.com), provides an enclosure that accepts bare SATA hard drives, and handles all the data exchange (and redundant backup) among the drives by itself. You can also connect a few drives via FireWire and configure them as a RAID using Apple's Disk Utility, or the $130 SoftRAID (www.softraid.com).

Figure 8.19 iMovie recognizes movie files in your iPhoto library.

Importing Other Movies

Although iMovie is designed to import footage from camcorders, it can also handle video from other video sources.

Importing movies from iPhoto

Movies you shoot using a digital still camera can be imported into iPhoto, making it the best route to bring such videos into iMovie.

To import movies from iPhoto:

1. In the Event List, select iPhoto Videos (**Figure 8.19**).

2. Locate a video clip in the list.

3. Drag the file to the Project Browser (see "Adding Clips to the Movie" in Chapter 10).

Importing video from old iMovie projects

Projects created in iMovie '08 share the same format as those in iMovie '09, so you can open and edit them directly. iMovie '09 can also import projects created in iMovie HD, but the results aren't what you may be hoping for. Basically, you'll get the raw footage with some basic editing applied (which is why you should finish any old projects in iMovie HD).

To import video from old iMovie projects:

1. From the File menu, choose Import > iMovie HD Project.

2. Locate an iMovie HD project; if it's a 1080i project, choose whether to import the footage as Large or Full.

3. Click Import. The video is imported to the Event Browser, and the contents of the Timeline appear in the Project Browser; any transitions are converted to Cross Dissolve transitions.

IMPORTING OTHER MOVIES

Importing movie files

iMovie is built on QuickTime, Apple's technology for playing and creating all sorts of digital audio and video, so you can import movie files into your projects.

To import a movie file into iMovie:

◆ Drag a QuickTime-compatible movie file from the Finder to an Event name in the Event Browser (**Figure 8.20**). Note that this action *moves* the file from its original location to the iMovie Events folder where the program stores its clips. If you'd rather *copy* the file, hold the Option key as you drag.

Or

1. In iMovie, choose Import Movies from the File menu.

2. Locate the file in the dialog and choose an Event (or create a new Event).

3. At the bottom of the dialog, choose whether to copy or move the original movie file to iMovie's preferred location (**Figure 8.21**).

4. Click the Import button. The clip appears in the Event you specified.

✔ Tips

■ The iMovie help files state that only QuickTime (.mov), MPEG-4, and DV formatted files can be imported, but several other formats that QuickTime supports appear to import fine.

■ Most movie files are small in size and compressed, which is great for viewing on the Web but not so good-looking compared to a DV clip taken from a video camcorder (**Figure 8.22**).

Figure 8.20 Add a QuickTime-compatible movie to your project by dragging it to the Event list.

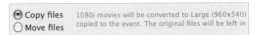

Figure 8.21 If you import movies using the dialog, be sure to choose whether the files are copied or moved.

Figure 8.22 To compare image resolution, I exported some DV footage (top) as a QuickTime file suitable for Web playback, and then imported the file back into iMovie (bottom).

IMPORTING OTHER MOVIES

Importing Footage from an Analog Camcorder

The process of importing footage from an analog camcorder in iMovie is much the same as when importing from a digital camcorder. However, you need a go-between device that converts the camcorder's analog signal to digital information on the Mac. Products from companies such as Canopus (www.canopus.com) or ADS Technologies (www.adstech.com) feature a FireWire or USB port for connecting to your computer and RCA-style inputs for connecting to your camera; some devices also include an S-Video port.

To import from a non-DV camcorder:

1. Connect the conversion device to the Mac and to the camera using RCA or S-Video cabling.

2. Switch the camcorder to VCR or Play mode.

3. Bring up the Import window in iMovie, choose or create an Event, and click the Import button.

4. Push the camcorder's Play button.

5. When finished, click the Stop button to finish capturing video, and press the Stop button on the camcorder.

✔ Tip

■ Since you're importing converted analog data, iMovie doesn't automatically split clips according to scenes. You'll have to use iMovie's editing tools to trim and organize the clips, or manually start and stop importing according to scenes.

Importing Old VHS Tapes Using a DV Camcorder

If you own a digital camcorder, but still have some older VHS (or other format) tapes, you can bring that footage into iMovie to edit or even just to store digitally. Connect your VCR to your camcorder and record the contents of the VHS tape to the DV tape. Then you can import your footage into iMovie normally. (Or, use an analog-to-digital converter between the VCR and your Mac.)

Another option is to use a recent Sony DV camcorder, which performs an in-camera analog-to-digital conversion.

Analog tape doesn't last forever—save your wedding/graduation/school play on disk. As a gift to my wife on our tenth wedding anniversary, I digitized the video from the ceremony (shot by my uncle on VHS), cut together the highlights, and burned it to a DVD. I'm glad I did—the image and sound quality had severely deteriorated (**Figure 8.23**).

Figure 8.23 The quality of VHS tapes deteriorates, as evidenced by this 15-year-old captured frame. (The damage is more dramatic full-size; see it at www.jeffcarlson.com/imovievqs/vhs.html.)

Extracting Footage from a DVD

So you burned a movie to DVD last year and want to snag some of that footage without trying to find the original MiniDV tape. Cinematize (www.miraizon.com), and DropDV (www.dropdv.com) can each extract the MPEG-2 video files stored on DVD discs. You can then import the footage into iMovie. DropDV is the more straightforward option, so I'll use that as the example program here.

To extract video from a DVD:

1. Insert a DVD into your Mac. If the DVD Player application launches, quit it.

2. Open the DVD's volume on the Desktop and locate the folder called VIDEO_TS.

3. Open the VIDEO_TS folder and locate the MPEG video files, which end in the suffix .VOB (**Figure 8.24**).

4. Drag the .VOB file onto DropDV. Depending on the movie's length, the conversion process could take a while (**Figure 8.25**).

5. Drag the .DV file that was created to your iMovie project to add it.

✔ Tips

- Keep in mind that video you pull from a DVD is compressed, and will therefore be of lower quality than the original. But sometimes that's better than not having any footage at all.

- If you're importing an MPEG video and it has no sound, convert it using the free MPEG Streamclip (www.squared5.com).

- Be good, use copyrighted video footage legally, and only extract video from discs you own or have the rights to use. You know the drill.

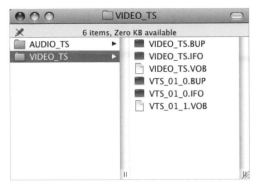

Figure 8.24 Video and audio on a DVD are stored in the VIDEO_TS folder as .VOB files.

Figure 8.25 DropDV converts MPEG-2 formatted video files to DV files in a minimal interface.

Copy-protected DVDs

Some DVD extraction utilities won't work with commercial DVDs that have copy protection applied, but there's a workaround. Download the free utility HandBrake (handbrake.fr) to pull even "secure" footage off most discs. (The latest version also requires a utility called VLC to perform its magic.)

Obviously, I'm not advocating movie piracy here. But there are legitimate occasions when you might want to use a section of a movie (in a multimedia school report, for example), or copy a movie that you own to your laptop's hard drive to watch later without toting along a sleeve of discs when you travel.

9

MANAGING VIDEO

Now that you've imported all that video, what are you going to do with it? Make a movie, of course, and it's likely you've already done so (if you followed the steps in Chapter 6).

But what if your movie is more complex than a short uploaded to YouTube? What if you're faced with hours and hours of footage that needs to be culled and sorted before you can even begin to think about building the good clips into a movie? What if you want to find clips from an old project?

iMovie '09 includes powerful features for viewing, classifying, and keeping track of your footage—including several advanced capabilities that are initially hidden.

Skimming Video

iMovie employs two methods of displaying the contents of clips. One is displaying the filmstrip as a series of thumbnail images (see Chapter 7). Another is skimming.

To skim a clip:

1. Position the mouse pointer over a clip (in either the Project or Event Browser). The vertical red playhead indicates the current frame, which is displayed in the Viewer (**Figure 9.1**).

2. Drag the pointer left or right across the clip. As you drag, the playhead moves and the Viewer previews that section of the clip (**Figure 9.2**).

   The benefit to this approach is that you can drag at whatever speed you like—you don't have to use VCR-style controls to rewind or fast-forward through the video.

Audio skimming

As you move the playhead, the audio plays at whatever speed you're moving the mouse pointer. (Sometimes that's helpful to gauge overall volume, but I find it distracting.)

To enable or disable audio skimming:

◆ Click the Audio Skimming button, choose Audio Skimming from the View menu, or press Command-K (**Figure 9.3**). The audio level indicators continue to display the volume levels but you won't hear the sound. (The sound is audible when playing clips normally.)

✔ Tips

■ Press the Control key to move the pointer over footage without skimming.

■ When you reach the right edge of a line in the Project Browser, hold Shift to jump down to the next line.

Playhead

Figure 9.1 When you skim a clip (bottom), the frame under the playhead appears in the Viewer (top).

Figure 9.2 This is the same clip as above, but skimming allows us to view the frames later in the clip (in this case, a pan across the landscape).

Audio Skimming button

Figure 9.3 Click the Audio Skimming button to toggle audio playback while skimming.

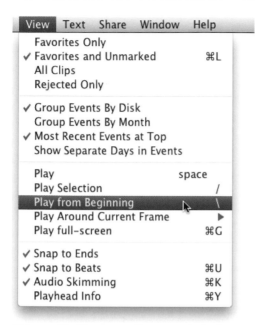

Figure 9.4 The View menu offers more playback options beyond just simply playing the movie.

Play button (Project Library)

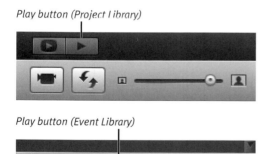

Play button (Event Library)

Figure 9.5 The Play buttons located below the Project Library and Event Library play video from the beginning of either section's filmstrip.

Playing Video

When I talk about "playing," I'm referring to watching video in real time. Naturally, you can play a clip or movie from start to finish. iMovie also provides a few approaches to watching selected clips or just a few frames near the playhead—good for when you're fine-tuning an edit or transition. And, of course, you can view your video in full-screen mode for that almost-cinematic experience. (If you sit real close to the monitor, it's just like being in a theater...a very tiny, empty theater, but with less expensive popcorn!)

To play video:

◆ Position the playhead in a clip and press the spacebar. The video appears in the Viewer.

◆ To play a filmstrip from its beginning, no matter where the playhead is located, press the \ (backslash) key or choose Play from Beginning from the View menu (**Figure 9.4**).

You can also click the Play button in either the Project Library or the Event Library, depending on which footage you want to play (**Figure 9.5**).

To play selected video:

1. Click and drag to select a range of frames.

2. Press either the spacebar or the / (forward-slash) key, or choose Play Selection from the View menu. Playback stops at the end of the selection.

PLAYING VIDEO

To play around the current frame:

1. Position the playhead in a clip.

2. Do one of the following:
   - ▲ Press the [(left bracket) key to play 1 second around the playhead. iMovie starts playing from half a second before the playhead to half a second after the playhead (**Figure 9.6**).
   - ▲ Press the] (right bracket) to play 3 seconds around the playhead (1.5 seconds on either side).

To play video full screen:

1. Position the playhead in the filmstrip you want to watch.

2. Press Command-G, choose Play full-screen from the View menu, or press the Play Full Screen button located next to the Play button in either the Project Library or Event Library. iMovie fills the screen with your movie.

   In full-screen mode, you can also move the mouse pointer to reveal a filmstrip (**Figure 9.7**). This enables you to:
   - ▲ Press the Play/Pause button to stop playback, or click on the filmstrip.
   - ▲ When paused, drag to skim to any section of the video.
   - ▲ Press the right or left arrow keys to move the playhead one frame at a time.

3. Press the Esc key to exit full-screen mode.

✔ Tips

- ■ If you want full-screen mode to remain active at the end of the movie, open iMovie's preferences and disable Exit full-screen mode after playback is finished.

- ■ Also in preferences, choose an option from the Full-screen playback size pop-up menu to control the movie's resolution (**Figure 9.8**).

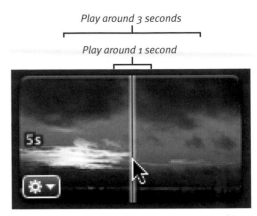

Figure 9.6 The Play Around feature lets you view the current frame in context without making you move the playhead manually. (This is a 5 second clip.)

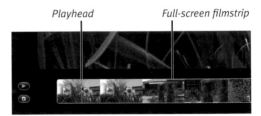

Figure 9.7 You can bring up a filmstrip and browse the movie without exiting full-screen mode.

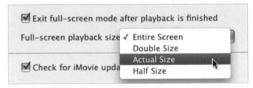

Figure 9.8 Choosing Actual Size from the pop-up menu offers a better reproduction of the movie's quality than Entire Screen, especially if you're working on a large display. However, you might not notice much difference if the video is high definition.

Double-click Behavior

In iMovie '09, double-clicking a clip brings up the Inspector. If you prefer a double-click to play a clip, as it was in iMovie '08, change the setting in the Browser pane of iMovie's preferences.

Handle   Selection border   Duration of selection

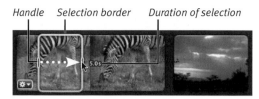

Figure 9.9 Click and drag to select a range of video.

Figure 9.10 Dragging a handle expands (or contracts) the selection.

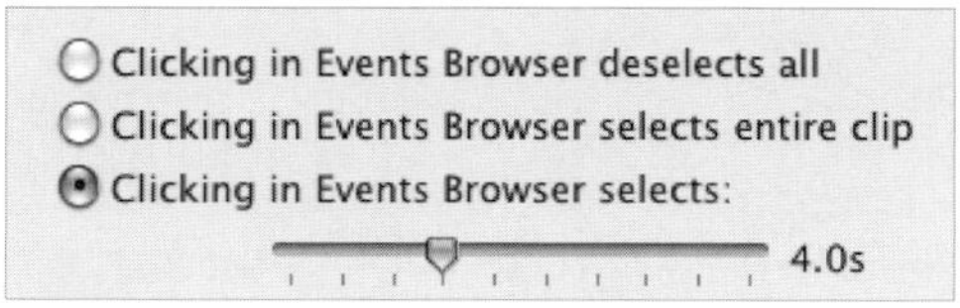

○ Clicking in Events Browser deselects all
○ Clicking in Events Browser selects entire clip
◉ Clicking in Events Browser selects:
    4.0s

Figure 9.11 These options dictate what happens when you single-click a clip in the Event Browser.

Selecting Video

Keep in mind that the filmstrip in iMovie is like a paragraph of text in a word processor. Just as you would highlight characters and words in text, you can select individual frames or full clips.

To select a portion of a clip:

◆ Click once on a clip. In the Event Browser, this automatically selects a four-second range of frames. (The duration can be changed; see below.) In the Project Browser, the entire clip is selected.

◆ Click and drag to select a custom range of frames, using the Viewer (which always shows the frame under the playhead) as a guide. The number to the right indicates the length of the selection (**Figure 9.9**).

To adjust a selection:

◆ Click and drag the handles on the edges of the selection box (**Figure 9.10**).

To change the default duration of a selection:

1. Open the preferences window by choosing Preferences from the iMovie menu, or by pressing Command-, (comma).

2. Choose one of the following options (**Figure 9.11**):
   ▲ **Clicking in Events Browser deselects all.** This option is helpful if you primarily drag to select frames and don't want iMovie to select for you.
   ▲ **Clicking in Events Browser selects entire clip.** This is self-explanatory; you can still select ranges by clicking and dragging.
   ▲ **Clicking in Events Browser selects:** Drag the slider to set a default length of time for the selection.

SELECTING VIDEO

To select an entire clip:

◆ With part of a clip selected, choose Select Entire Clip from the Edit menu, or press Command-A.

To select multiple clips:

1. Select a single clip or a portion of a clip.

2. Hold Shift and click another clip to include all the clips in between. Or, hold Command and click non-contiguous clips (**Figure 9.12**).

To deselect all clips:

◆ Choose Select None from the Edit menu, or press Command-Shift-A.

◆ Click an empty area in the browser (such as between clips).

Recentering video

Recentering (which is iMovie's term for an editing technique called *slipping*) is particularly useful when you're working with fixed time periods.

For example, suppose you select five seconds of footage at the beginning of a clip, but then realize that five seconds toward the clip's end would work better. Instead of separately adjusting the beginning and ending of your selection, simply recenter the clip.

To recenter a clip:

1. Make a selection.

2. Position the mouse pointer over the top or bottom of the yellow selection border. The cursor becomes a hand with an arrow in it (**Figure 9.13**).

3. Drag left or right to choose a new selection range without changing the selection's duration (**Figure 9.14**).

Figure 9.12 Command-clicking selected these non-contiguous clips. If I had Shift-clicked, all the clips would be selected.

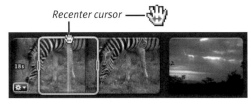

Figure 9.13 You know the cursor is positioned correctly to recenter the selection when you see a double-arrow icon appear within the hand.

Figure 9.14 After you've recentered the selection, the duration remains the same but different frames are included.

✔ Tips

■ With a selection made, you can expand or contract it by holding Shift and clicking a new frame of that clip instead of dragging the selection handles.

■ Choose Edit > Select to choose from more selection options, such as To Playhead (Shift-A) and all instances of specific elements (video clips, transitions, photos, maps, and backgrounds).

Add button

Figure 9.15 Click the Add button for a new project.

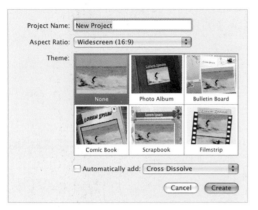

Figure 9.16 In addition to naming and choosing an aspect ratio for your project, you can apply a theme.

Figure 9.17 Folders let you group together related projects and reduce clutter.

Projects Intended for iPhone

You can share a movie of any size to an iPhone, but if you want to avoid black bars around the edges of the picture to account for the iPhone screen's 3:2 aspect ratio, and you know you want the movie to end up on an iPhone or iPod touch, choose iPhone when you create the project.

Managing Projects

iMovie '09 keeps track of all your projects in one place instead of asking you to open a new file for each one.

Creating a new project

When you create a new project, it appears in the Project Library. For easier organization, you can put projects into folders.

To create a new project:

1. Choose New Project from the File menu (or press Command-N). Or, if you're viewing the Project Library (click the Project Library button in the Project Browser), you can click the Add button (**Figure 9.15**).

2. In the dialog that appears (**Figure 9.16**), give the project a descriptive file name.

3. Choose an aspect ratio for the project. iMovie can accept several video formats and sizes, so pick the size you want the final movie to be. The project's aspect ratio can be changed later if you want (see the next page).

4. If you want to apply a theme to the project, click one of the thumbnails. You can choose to apply or remove a theme later if you prefer (see Chapter 14).

5. If you want iMovie to automatically create transitions between every clip to save you the trouble, enable the Automatically add button, and choose a transition style from the pop-up menu.

6. Click Create.

To organize projects into folders:

1. Choose New Folder from the File menu.

2. Name the folder in the dialog that appears.

3. Drag a project to the folder (**Figure 9.17**).

To change the aspect ratio in a project:

1. In the Project Library, select the project you want to change.

2. Choose Project Properties from the File menu, or press Command-J, to bring up the Project Properties dialog.

3. Choose a different option from the Aspect Ratio pop-up menu (**Figure 9.18**).

4. Click OK to apply the setting. iMovie automatically crops the footage to accommodate the new size (see Chapter 10 for more on cropping).

Duplicating and deleting projects

It's not uncommon to reach a fork in the editing road where you'd like to try a couple of different approaches. In that case, you can duplicate your project and work with a copy; if it doesn't work out as you hoped, simply go to the first version and delete the duplicate.

To duplicate a project:

1. Select a project in the Project Library.

2. Choose Duplicate Project from the File menu. You can also right-click or Control-click the project's name and choose Duplicate Project from the contextual menu that appears (**Figure 9.19**). A new version with a number appended (such as "My First Movie 1") is created.

To delete a project:

1. Select a project in the Project Library.

2. Choose Move Project to Trash from the File menu or the contextual menu, or press Command-Delete.

✔ Tip

■ Duplicating a project does not duplicate the media files on your hard disk. By the same token, deleting a project does not erase the media files on disk.

Figure 9.18 You can change a project's aspect ratio at any time.

Figure 9.19 Work on a copy of a project by duplicating it, in this case via the contextual menu.

NTSC and PAL

iMovie's preferences let you choose the video standard: either NTSC - 30 fps or PAL - 25 fps. The setting is located in the Video section and applies only after you restart iMovie.

MANAGING PROJECTS

Figure 9.20 Select two or more Events to merge them into one Event.

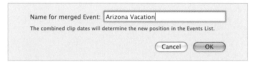

Figure 9.21 Provide a new Event name, since you're essentially creating one from scratch.

Figure 9.22 The sparse amount of Day 1 footage is now merged with the plentiful Day 2 video.

Figure 9.23 Select a clip that will be the first video in the new Event you create.

Figure 9.24 The clips following the split point now appear in their own Event, which iMovie labels with an incremental number.

Managing Events

When you import footage, iMovie's default behavior is to split each day's video into a separate Event (an option you can turn off during import; see Chapter 8). For more organizational control, you can merge or split Events.

For example, I have video from a recent trip where not much footage was shot on day one, but plenty was shot on the second day. I'd prefer to group them together as one Event.

To merge Events:

1. In the Event list, select the Events you wish to merge: Shift-click to select all Events between the ones you click, or Command-click to select discrete clips (**Figure 9.20**).

2. Choose Merge Events from the File menu, or Control-click and choose Merge Events from the contextual menu.

3. In the dialog that appears, type a name for the merged Event (**Figure 9.21**).

4. Click OK. The Events are merged into a single unit (**Figure 9.22**).

Similarly, you can split an Event to break out any content. In this example, I want a new Event for an excursion from the second day.

To split an Event:

◆ In the Event Browser, select a clip (or portion of a clip) and choose Split Event Before Selected Clip from the File menu or Split Event Before Clip from the contextual menu (**Figure 9.23**). All clips from that point to the end of the Event are moved into their own Event (**Figure 9.24**).

✔ Tip

■ You can split an Event using the contextual menu based on the position of the playhead without selecting a clip.

Moving Projects and Events to Other Drives

iMovie stores the footage you import and the projects you create on your Mac's internal hard disk by default, but you can move them easily to an external drive, freeing valuable hard disk space.

It's important to relocate projects and events *within iMovie*, even though the program is copying files in the Finder. If you move them manually, the links between the project clips and their source files can break.

To move a project to another drive:

1. In the Project Library, drag a project to the icon of another hard drive (**Figure 9.25**).

   This action normally *copies* the file, leaving the original in place. If you'd rather *move* the file, which deletes the original, hold Command while dragging (you won't see the green plus-sign icon on the mouse pointer).

2. In the dialog that appears, choose whether you want to copy or move just the project file or the project plus the event files (**Figure 9.26**).

   It's fine to store them on separate drives. For example, perhaps you've chosen to store raw video files on one external drive and the projects on another. But if one of the drives is offline, you won't be able to edit the footage.

This icon indicates more projects are listed below.

Figure 9.25 Drag a project to another hard drive's icon to move it.

Figure 9.26 Easily keep a project and its source footage together when you move the project.

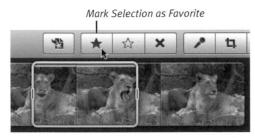

Mark Selection as Favorite

Figure 9.27 Mark a selection of video as a favorite to find it easily when you assemble your movie.

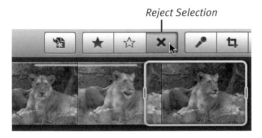

Reject Selection

Figure 9.28 Click the Reject Selection button to hide the selected footage from view (top). You can see that the clip is now shorter, based on the length of the green favorite line (bottom). If you position the mouse pointer over the clip, you will also see that the clip's duration has changed.

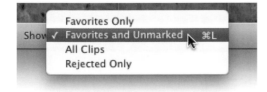

Figure 9.29 Choose an option for the Show pop-up menu to narrow the clips shown.

Marking Footage

You're bound to end up with footage that never ends up in a movie, so why trip over it every time you go to the Event Browser? By the same token, you can easily identify which clips are better than others. It's easy to mark footage as a favorite or reject it (without deleting it, just in case).

To mark video as a favorite:

1. In the Event Browser, select a range of video you like; it can be an entire clip, multiple clips, or a range of footage.

2. Click the Mark Selection as Favorite button or press F (**Figure 9.27**). A green bar appears at the top of the filmstrip.

To unmark video:

1. If you changed your mind about some favorited footage, select it.

2. Click the Unmark Selection button, or press U. The green bar disappears from that section.

To reject footage:

1. In the Event Browser, select a range of video you want to reject (**Figure 9.28**).

2. Click the Reject Selection button, or press R. Or, press the Delete key. That footage is hidden (but not permanently deleted).

To control which clips are visible in the Event Browser:

◆ From the Show pop-up menu at the bottom of the screen, choose one of the options (**Figure 9.29**). Only those clips appear in the browser.

MARKING FOOTAGE

Using advanced marking tools

The techniques on the previous page are already more useful than what was offered in earlier versions of iMovie—and yet those represent just the basic marking behavior. Enabling iMovie's advanced tools makes using the marking features faster.

To mark video (advanced):

1. In iMovie's preferences, make sure Show Advanced Tools is enabled (**Figure 9.30**). Two new buttons appear in the toolbar: the Arrow tool and the Keyword tool (**Figure 9.31**).

   The Arrow tool is necessary because the buttons change state. Normally, clicking a button immediately performs an action, but with the advanced tools enabled, clicking a button activates that tool in preparation for the action. So, when you're not using those tools, choose the Arrow tool.

2. Click the Favorite tool, Unmark tool, or Reject tool button to select it.

3. Click and drag across the footage you want to mark (**Figure 9.32**). Continue doing this for every section of video you want to mark or unmark, without switching tools.

✔ Tip

■ When iMovie is in advanced mode and you have a range of video selected, the tool buttons gain a plus sign (**Figure 9.33**). That indicates the buttons work as they do in normal mode: click a button to mark the clip.

Figure 9.30 Unlock advanced tools from within iMovie's preferences.

Arrow tool   *Keyword tool*

Figure 9.31 These options dictate what happens when you single-click a clip in the Event Browser.

Marking footage as a favorite

Rejecting footage

Figure 9.32 Simply dragging a selection with the advanced Favorite tool makes it a favorite, versus making a selection and then clicking the button. The actions are color-coded to easily show if you're rejecting footage instead (bottom).

Unmark Selection

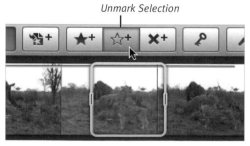

Figure 9.33 If a section of frames is already selected, the toolbar buttons revert to their normal behavior.

MARKING FOOTAGE

Figure 9.34 iMovie adds a bright red bar and title in the browser to indicate that this is the reject bin.

Working with Rejected Footage

Remember that iMovie isn't actually deleting any file from your hard disk, only keeping track of which portions of clips have been rejected. You can retrieve the footage at any point, or send it to the Trash if you're sure you won't need it.

To retrieve rejected footage:

1. From the Show menu below the Event Browser, choose Rejected Only. The browser displays only rejected footage with an extra heading titled Rejected Clips (**Figure 9.34**).

2. Select a clip or a range of frames that you want to retrieve.

3. Click the Unmark button.

✔ Tips

- If you're using advanced mode, click the Unmark button and then drag across the portions you wish to retrieve.

- You can also retrieve a rejected clip by marking it as a Favorite.

- Another option is to move footage directly to a Project by clicking the Add to Project button (see the next chapter for more information). When you do this, however, the rejected footage remains marked as rejected; only a copy is sent to the project. Furthermore, when that clip is in a project but the source clip is marked as rejected, iMovie will not move rejected clips to the Trash.

- Levels of Undo don't transfer between your editing sessions. When you quit iMovie and then launch it again later, your last actions are forgotten.

How iMovie manages clips on your hard disk

At some point you'll decide to really get rid of the rejected clips, not just hide them from view. But before I get into the specifics of sending clips to the Trash on the next page, it's important to understand how iMovie works with the video files stored on your hard disk.

When you import footage, iMovie creates a new clip for each scene, which also adds a new clip file to your hard disk. However, even if you split, duplicate, or otherwise edit a clip in iMovie, *the media file stays the same* (**Figure 9.35**). iMovie actually records only the *changes* made to the clip, and doesn't alter the clip's original media file.

This clip management style comes in handy in several ways as you use iMovie.

Advantages of iMovie's method of managing clips:

◆ **Undo.** iMovie offers virtually unlimited levels of Undo during an editing session, enabling you to recombine split clips, remove effects that have been applied, and other actions.

◆ **Deleting clips.** When you trim a clip and throw away one of the portions (described in Chapter 10), that discarded section can be pulled from the piece you kept.

◆ **Use the same footage in multiple projects.** Add a scene to several movie projects without duplicating the source file on disk. iMovie only needs to reference the original copy.

✔ Tip

■ That series of numbers in the media file indicates the date and time the clip was shot. The clip in Figure 9.35 was captured at 11:38:22 a.m. on November 27, 2005 (I guess I'm overdue for another vacation!).

clip-2005-11-27
11;38;22.dv

Figure 9.35 The original clip on disk, "clip-2005-11-27 11;38;22.dv," was split into three separate clips, but the source file located on the hard disk is not renamed or split.

iMovie File Locations

You may never need to worry about where the files are located, but if the situation comes up, here's the rundown.

iMovie's files are located in the Movies folder of your Home folder. Inside the Movies folder are three other folders:

◆ **iMovie Events.** The original movie files you import end up here, within separate folders for each Event.

◆ **iMovie Projects.** These are the data files that keep track of which footage is used and which edits are applied.

◆ **iMovie Sharing.** When you share a movie to iTunes, YouTube, or the Media Browser, the exported versions are stored here.

Before   After

Figure 9.36 After moving the rejected portion of a clip to the Trash, iMovie rewrites the original file to account for the deleted footage.

Rescuing Clips via Time Machine

Mac OS X's Time Machine feature backs up any files on your hard disk that have changed in the past hour. Though you may have sent part of a clip to the Trash and then emptied it (which rewrites the source clip), the original is probably still available.

To restore a clip using Time Machine:

1. Quit iMovie.

2. Click Time Machine in the Dock.

3. Type the name of the clip you're locating in the Finder window's search field. Or, use the timeline at right or the back and forward arrow buttons to browse the save states.

4. When you've found the version of the file you want, select it and click the Restore button. The file is copied to its original folder.

5. Launch iMovie, which rebuilds the Event's thumbnails and includes the formerly deleted clip.

Sending clips to the Trash

If you know (if you're *certain*) you're not going to need any of the deleted clips later, you can move clips marked as rejected to the Trash. (To be clear, this is the Trash found in the Finder; unlike iMovie HD and earlier versions, iMovie '09 does not include a trash within the program.)

To move rejected clips to the Trash:

1. From the File menu, choose Move Rejected Clips to Trash.

2. In the dialog that appears, click the Move to Trash button. If you click View Rejected Clips, iMovie displays only the rejected footage in the Event Browser (as described two pages ago).

   The clip disappears from the Event Browser, and its source file is rewritten so that it contains only the remaining video (**Figure 9.36**).

   Even though the clip seems to be gone from iMovie, you can still choose Undo from the Edit menu to bring it back at this point.

3. To free up the space on the hard disk, go to the Finder and choose Empty Trash from the Finder menu. Now it's really gone (well, with one caveat; see the side-bar at left).

✔ Tip

■ Rather than risk deleting video accidentally, I make a point of never moving rejected footage to the Trash until a project is completely finished—maybe not even then, if you have enough available disk space.

Using iMovie's Space Saver

We're jumping ahead a little here, but when you've finished editing a project, you can use iMovie's Space Saver feature to remove footage and reduce clutter in the Event Library.

To remove footage using Space Saver:

1. Select one or more events you want to clean up in the Event list.

2. Choose Space Saver from the File menu.

3. In the dialog that appears, choose which types of footage are to be moved to the Trash: video that doesn't appear in any projects, video that's currently unmarked, and video not marked with a keyword (**Figure 9.37**).

4. Click the Reject and Review button to continue. iMovie displays the Rejected Clips view in the Event Browser so you can double-check which clips are going to be deleted.

5. Click Move Rejected to Trash to delete the clips from the Event Library.

✔ Tips

■ Don't forget that even if you empty the Trash, you may still have a backup of your clips: if you shot with a tape-based camcorder, the original footage is stored on the source tape.

■ If you don't use Time Machine, a regular backup system should enable you to restore files that have been deleted. See Joe Kissell's *Take Control of Mac OS X Backups* (www.takecontrolbooks.com/backup-macosx.html).

Figure 9.37 Space Saver automates a process that would take too long to do by hand.

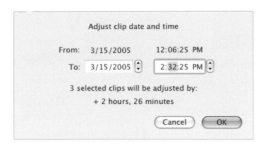

Figure 9.38 Correct bad timecode capture using the Adjust clip date and time feature.

Changing Clip Dates and Times

A camcorder marks every clip with the date and time of capture (invisibly, not with the little digital clock that appeared on videos of old). But that assumes the camcorder is set with the correct date and time. What if you're working with two video sources (such as a wedding) and one camera's time is off? A new feature in iMovie '09 can help.

To change clip dates:

1. Select one or more clips that need changing in the Event Browser.

2. Choose Adjust clip date and time from the File menu or the contextual menu.

3. In the dialog that appears, change the date, time, or both (**Figure 9.38**).

Assigning Keywords

One curious omission in iMovie is the capability to name clips, a feature in early versions that helped you determine what scenes a clip contained. The filmstrip and skimming made naming clips mostly unnecessary. However, you don't want to search your entire Event Library visually.

iMovie's keyword feature goes far beyond naming clips. Keywords are part of iMovie's advanced tools, so if you're not seeing the options I describe here, make sure the Show Advanced Tools option is enabled in iMovie's preferences.

To assign keywords using Auto-Apply:

1. Click the Keyword tool or press K to bring up the Keyword window (**Figure 9.39**), and click the Auto-Apply button if it's not already selected.

2. Select the checkboxes of the keywords you want to apply (**Figure 9.40**). You can also enable or disable them quickly by pressing the numbers 1 through 9 (keywords in the slots for 10 and above don't get keyboard shortcuts).

3. In the Event Browser, drag to select the range of frames to which you want to assign the keywords (**Figure 9.41**). A blue line appears in the filmstrip to indicate where keywords are applied.

To assign keywords using the Keywords Inspector:

1. Taking the opposite approach, first use the Arrow tool to select a range of frames you want to tag with keywords.

2. Click the Keyword tool (or press K); the Inspector button is already selected.

3. Click keywords to apply them (or press their number key equivalents).

Keyword tool

Figure 9.39 The Keyword tool appears when Show Advanced Tools is enabled in iMovie's preferences.

Figure 9.40 A number of keywords are set up initially to get you started.

Keyword applied

Figure 9.41 As with marking favorites or rejects in advanced mode, drag to apply keywords to selected footage.

ASSIGNING KEYWORDS

Figure 9.42 Create keywords that reflect the content of your own footage (Inspector view shown here).

Figure 9.43 iMovie keeps track of which keywords have been applied.

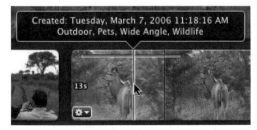

Figure 9.44 Keywords appear at the bottom of the Playhead Info display.

To create a new keyword:

1. Type a word or phrase into the New Keyword field.

2. Click the Add or Add to Clip button (depending on which view is active), or press Return (**Figure 9.42**). The keyword appears in the list.

To remove keywords:

1. In the Auto-Apply view, click to select one or more keywords in the list.

2. Click the Remove button. If the keyword has been applied to footage, iMovie verifies that you want to remove it from the clips (**Figure 9.43**). Click Yes.

To rename keywords:

1. Double-click a keyword in the list.

2. Type a new keyword in its place. If the keyword has been applied, iMovie asks if you want to change it. Click Yes.

✔ Tips

- To quickly apply keywords to an entire clip, select the Keyword tool and Option-click a clip.

- Rearrange the entries in the Keywords Inspector by dragging them up or down in the list.

- To see which keywords are applied to a clip, choose Playhead Info from the View menu. The keywords appear in addition to the capture date and time (**Figure 9.44**).

- If you think you'll use only a few keywords, delete the others and keep your list at nine items or less. Then you can use the number keys to apply keywords without even looking at the Keyword window.

ASSIGNING KEYWORDS

Viewing clips according to keywords

Once you've assigned keywords to your clips, it's much easier to locate just the footage you need.

To filter the Event Browser by keyword:

1. Display the Keyword Filter pane by choosing Show Keyword Filter from the Window menu, or by clicking the Keyword Filter button that becomes visible when you enable advanced tools (**Figure 9.45**).

2. Click the buttons to the left of the key-words you want to filter (**Figure 9.46**):

   ▲ **Green** (the right side) instructs iMovie to *show* just the clips with the applicable keywords.

   ▲ **Red** (the left side) *hides* clips that contain the selected keywords.

3. Choose a filtering logic:

   ▲ **Any** applies the filter to any clip with that keyword.

   ▲ **All** applies the filter only to clips that contain all of the keywords that are selected.

✔ Tips

■ When you hide the Keyword Filter pane, the filtering no longer applies.

■ After keywords are set up, you can turn off the advanced mode and still filter your footage. The keywords no longer appear in the Playhead Info display and the blue bars disappear. However, you can still view the Keyword Filter pane (choose Show Keyword Filter from the Window menu) and apply the filtering logic.

Keyword Filter pane button

Figure 9.45 The Keyword Filter pane provides another level of choosing which clips will appear.

No filter applied   *People keyword*

Figure 9.46 Selecting the People keyword with the selectors set to *exclude any* causes the clip of the man (top) to disappear (middle). Setting it to *include* results in just the People clips appearing (bottom).

"People" clips excluded

"People" clips included

Figure 9.47 Betcha never expected to see a Print dialog in iMovie.

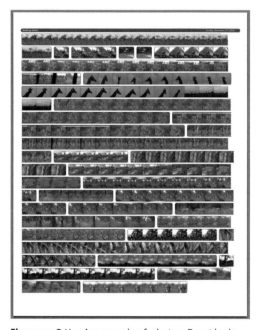

Figure 9.48 Here's a sample of what an Event looks like printed, in this case with the clip size slider set to 1s (1 second) and the thumbnail size slider set at about 25 percent of full size.

Printing an Event

Print? As in, on paper? Aren't we dealing with *video* here? While printing almost sounds like an outdated concept, iMovie offers the capability to make a hard copy version of an Event's footage for people who prefer to review information on paper.

To print an Event:

1. Select one or more items in the Event list.

2. Choose Print Event from the File menu, or press Command-P. The Print dialog appears (**Figure 9.47**).

3. In the iMovie portion of the dialog, choose a preferred number of pages, which dictates the size of the filmstrip thumbnails.

4. If you want to be able to see keywords and clip markings, enable the Show metadata checkbox.

5. Click Print to send the job to your printer. The end result uses the Event Browser's view settings (such as thumbnail size and number of thumbnails per second) to generate the printout (**Figure 9.48**).

10

EDITING VIDEO

The first movies were pure documentaries. Armed with new technology, camera operators shot what they saw: trains leaving the station, people at work, the movement of animals. Motion pictures didn't need to tell a story because the story was in the reproduction. The first movie created by brothers Louis and Auguste Lumière was the action spectacular *Workers Leaving the Lumière Factory*, depicting exactly that.

However, filmmakers soon realized their "flickers" didn't need to be just linear slices of life. They could shoot movies in any order and assemble them to tell a story, or even combine totally unrelated scenes for dramatic effect. Lev Kuleshov, an early Russian filmmaker, filmed a closeup of an actor wearing a neutral expression. He then intercut a scene of an empty bowl, prompting audiences to praise the actor's subtle portrayal of hunger. Kuleshov took the same neutral footage and intercut scenes of a dead woman in a coffin, then a girl playing with a doll, and in each case audiences were amazed to see the actor's grief or joy. Editing became a vehicle for expressing emotions or ideas that weren't necessarily present during filming.

Today, iMovie and non-linear editing give you the capability to use the visual language of film to tell stories, whether fiction or simply a day at the park. The fun begins here!

Time and Timecode

In Chapter 2, I explained how timecode works as it applies to a camcorder. In iMovie, time is displayed as fractions of seconds by default. If you're more comfortable with traditional timecode, which expresses individual frames instead of seconds, you can switch to that display. Either way, you'll find time displayed in several areas.

To enable timecode display:

1. Choose Preferences from the iMovie menu to open the preferences window, or press Command-, (comma).

2. Select the checkbox labeled Display Time as HH:MM:SS:Frames, and then close the window.

Time and Timecode in iMovie

◆ **At the Playhead (Project Browser).** When the Playhead Info display is active (choose Playhead Info from the View menu), it always shows the time relative to the entire movie in your project. So, for example, positioning the playhead two seconds into a clip that appears in the middle of your movie displays something like "8:14" (in seconds) or "0:08:04" (in timecode) instead of "2s" or "0:02:00" (**Figure 10.1**).

◆ **Beneath the Project Library and the Event Library.** In addition to showing timecode of individual clips, the total length of a project or Event appears below the relevant browser (**Figure 10.2**).

◆ **With a selection.** When you drag to select a range of frames, iMovie displays the duration next to the selection box as well as below the browser (**Figure 10.3**).

Playhead location in Playhead Info display

Figure 10.1 The playhead display refers to time location within the context of the movie, not within the clip. Time is shown here in seconds.

Playhead location   *Total movie length*

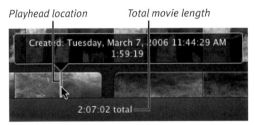

Figure 10.2 The duration of the filmstrip appears below the browser (the Project Library, in this case). Time is shown here in timecode.

Selection relative to total   *Selection duration*

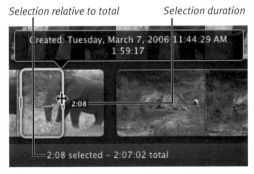

Figure 10.3 Selecting a range of frames offers more information.

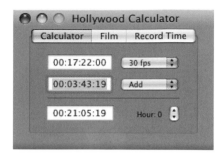

Figure 10.4 Hollywood Calculator is a free tool for handling timecode math.

✔ Tips

- When you select multiple clips, their combined duration appears below the browser.

- Need to quickly figure out the total length of your movie if you add a 3:43:19 clip to it? Plug it into Hollywood Calculator (www.happypixelstudios.com/hwcalc/), a free utility (**Figure 10.4**). Timecode math has never been easier.

- See "Understanding Timecode" in Chapter 2 for a timecode refresher.

Working through the Video Editing Backlog

One of the most common laments among home videographers is the backlog of footage that piles up, unedited. It's easy to shoot hours of video of your kids or vacation, but editing it into movies takes even more hours. I know people who have so many filled MiniDV tapes that they end up not editing any of it because the task is so huge.

The trick is to break down the editing into smaller components, so that it's not such an intimidating endeavor. Instead of facing an entire video that needs to be finished, approach the process in steps. You can tackle a step each weekend, for example. Here's one suggested approach.

1. In the Event Library, delete any full clips you know you won't ever use, such as the times when you didn't know the camera was on (yep, everyone does it). Don't try to edit out portions of clips; this step is just to remove the obvious deadwood.

2. Assemble a rough cut by dragging clips from the Event Browser to the Project Browser in the approximate order you want them to appear in the movie.

3. Start culling the obviously useless footage from your clips using the techniques described in this chapter.

4. Tighten your movie by trimming clips, paying attention to how it's paced. Start adding music and other additional audio.

5. With a tight edit in place, start applying transitions, titles, and effects.

6. Wrap up any final trimming and polishing.

See, it's not that intimidating after all!

TIME AND TIMECODE

Adding Clips to the Movie

Even with lots of clips in the Event Library, your movie doesn't exist until you begin building it in the Project Browser.

To add clips to the movie:

1. Select one or more clips or a range of footage in the Event Browser.

2. Do one of the following:
   ▲ Drag the selection to the Project Browser (**Figure 10.5**).
   ▲ Click the Add button or press the E key.

   The footage appears in your project's filmstrip (**Figure 10.6**). In the Event Browser, the section of video you added is indicated by an orange bar so you can quickly see which clips are used in a movie.

3. Add more clips to fill out a rough assembly of your movie.

To add clips (advanced mode):

1. Click the Edit tool (normally the Add Selection to Project button) or press E.

2. Drag to select the range of frames that will appear in the project (**Figure 10.7**). The selection appears as a new clip when you release the mouse button.

✔ Tips

- Option-click a clip with the Edit tool selected (in advanced mode) to add an entire clip to the movie.

- Command-click a clip in advanced mode to add just a four-second portion of the clip (the default duration can be set in iMovie's preferences).

- If you marked favorite scenes (see Chapter 9), choose Favorites Only from the Show pop-up menu, select all clips in the Event Browser, and then add them at once.

Add Selection to Project button

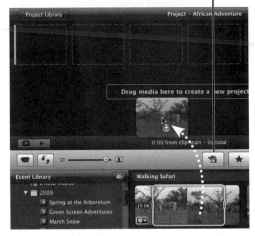

Figure 10.5 Add the footage to your project by dragging it to the Project Browser or clicking the Add Selection to Project button. (Me, I prefer to press E.)

Footage added to project

Clip in Event Browser indicates which footage is being used in a project.

Figure 10.6 Congratulations, you've just created a movie!

Figure 10.7 With the advanced tools enabled, just drag over your chosen footage to add it to the movie.

Figure 10.8 A pop-up menu with several options appears when you drop a clip onto another clip.

Figure 10.9 The original clip now appears as two clips surrounding the newly inserted clip.

Figure 10.10 The 4-second clip at top is replaced by an 8-second clip at bottom.

Inserting clips

Normally, adding a clip to your project positions it alongside other existing clips. But you can also insert a clip in the middle of another piece of footage.

To insert a clip:

1. Drag a clip from the Event Browser and release the mouse button when the playhead is in the middle of a clip.

2. From the pop-up menu that appears, choose Insert (**Figure 10.8**). The existing clip is split and the new footage appears between the breaks (**Figure 10.9**).

Replacing clips

It's common to throw together a rough edit and then realize another clip would be better than one in your project. Using iMovie's replace edits, you can easily swap the old clip for the new.

To replace a clip:

1. Drag a clip from the Event Browser and release the mouse button when the playhead is in the middle of a clip.

2. From the pop-up menu that appears, choose Replace. The old clip is removed and the new clip appears in its place.

✔ Tips

- The Replace command doesn't pay attention to duration. If you're replacing a 4-second clip with an 8-second one, the full eight seconds of footage appear (**Figure 10.10**). If you want to keep the original clip's duration, use the advanced replace commands on the next page.

- If you decide later to move a clip that you inserted, the two pieces of the split clip can be rejoined (see "Splitting clips" later in this chapter).

To replace a clip (advanced mode):

1. Make sure Show Advanced Tools is enabled in iMovie's preferences.

2. Drag a clip from the Event Browser and release the mouse button when the playhead is in the middle of a clip.

3. From the pop-up menu that appears (**Figure 10.11**), choose one of the following options. Unlike a straightforward Replace operation, these edits retain the original clip's duration (**Figure 10.12**).

   ▲ **Replace from Start.** The first frame of your selected clip becomes the first frame of the replacement clip.

   ▲ **Replace from End.** The last frame of your selection becomes the last frame of the replaced clip.

   ▲ **Replace at Playhead.** The first frame of your selection appears at the spot where you release the mouse button (**Figure 10.13**). iMovie grabs footage outside your selection if necessary to fill the space in the project, or makes the clip shorter if that's not possible.

Figure 10.11 With iMovie's advanced tools enabled, the pop-up menu offers several more options.

Replace from Start

Replace from End

Figure 10.12 The orange bar at the bottom of the 13-second clip in the Event Browser indicates which footage replaces the 10-second clip in Figure 10.11.

Replace at Playhead

Event Browser

Figure 10.13 In this example, I'm replacing the clip in Figure 10.11 with a 5-second selection (top) and choosing Replace at Playhead. iMovie adds frames from before the selection (compare the orange bar to the selection) to fill out the entire 10-second clip.

Music and Sound Effects Browser

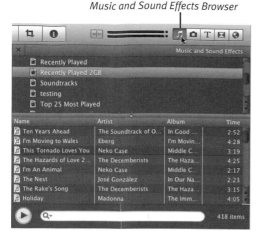

Figure 10.14 Choose a song in the Music and Sound Effects Browser.

Figure 10.15 Drag a beat marker to the audio clip.

Figure 10.16 Beat markers define the clips' durations when you add the footage to your project.

Editing Using Beat Markers

If you know you want to set your movie to a song, like a music video, iMovie offers a cool method of building the project. Using beat markers, you start with the song first, then let iMovie do all the cutting as you add clips. (See Chapter 12 for more on working with audio clips.)

To edit using beat markers:

1. Choose New Project from the File menu to start a new project.

2. Enable Snap to Beats under the View menu if it's not already active.

3. Open the Music and Sound Effects Browser (press Command-1 or click the button on the toolbar) and choose a song to use (**Figure 10.14**).

4. Drag the song to the Project Browser to add it as a background music track.

5. Click the song's Action menu and choose Clip Trimmer to open it.

6. Add beat markers using one of the following techniques:
   - ▲ Using the waveforms as a guide, drag the Beat Marker icon to the clip to create a new marker (**Figure 10.15**).
   - ▲ Begin playing the song (press the spacebar or the backslash (\) key), and then press the B key whenever you want a beat marker to appear. Don't worry about hitting every beat; you can reposition markers later.

7. With the beats in place, click Done to close the Clip Trimmer.

8. Add video clips to the project, either individually or in groups. iMovie automatically trims them to fit the spaces between beat markers (**Figure 10.16**).

To reposition beat markers:

1. Select the background music clip and open it in the Clip Trimmer.

2. Drag a beat marker to a new location (**Figure 10.17**). iMovie automatically adjusts the affected clips' durations to accommodate the change.

3. When you're done adjusting the beat markers, click Done in the Clip Trimmer.

To remove a beat marker:

1. Drag a beat marker out of the Clip Trimmer.

2. iMovie needs to compensate for the loss of the marker, so choose an action from the dialog that appears (**Figure 10.18**).

   ▲ Extend Left removes the video clip to the left of the marker and increases the duration of the clip to the right.

   ▲ Extend Right removes the clip to the right and increases the duration of the clip to the left.

   ▲ Leave As-Is keeps the video clips unchanged.

✔ Tips

■ If you add a new beat marker to the background track, the video clip in that position is split.

■ If you delete a video clip in the Project Browser, iMovie gives you a warning (**Figure 10.19**). Clicking Continue disables the Snap to Beat feature for beat markers after that point. A better alternative is to replace the clip using iMovie's advanced options to keep the overall duration the same.

Before move

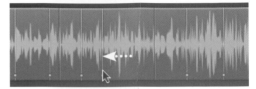

After move

Figure 10.17 After you drag the beat marker, the clip to the left is shortened and the clip to the right is extended.

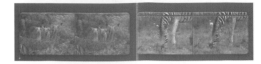

Figure 10.18 Choose how to deal with the removal of a beat marker.

Figure 10.19 Deleting a clip in the Project Browser can throw off the rest of the project.

EDITING USING BEAT MARKERS

Figure 10.20 Drag and drop to reorder clips.

Ordering Clips

The movie's order progresses from left to right, top to bottom (like reading a book) in the Project Browser. You can drag and drop clips into whatever order you choose.

To order clips:

1. Select a clip.

2. Drag the selection to a new location within the filmstrip. Depending on where you release the mouse button, one of two things happens:

   ▲ When you drag to the space between clips, a green bar appears to indicate the point at which the clip will end up (**Figure 10.20**).

   ▲ If you release the mouse when the playhead is in the middle of a clip, the pop-up menu appears with possible actions you can take, such as inserting or replacing the clip.

✔ Tips

- You can only reorder full clips in the Project Browser, not sections of clips. This limitation is easily worked around by editing the clip you want to move (detailed in the next several pages). However, at this point in the editing process, don't get hung up on moving individual sections of clips; you're working in broad strokes for now.

- You can also copy or cut a selected clip, move the playhead to a new location, and paste the clip. See "Copying and pasting clips," later in this chapter.

- As editor, you have power over time. Clips can appear in any order, no matter when the events happened chronologically. (Most studio movies are rarely—if ever—shot in chronological order.)

Multi-Touch Editing

If you're using a recent MacBook, MacBook Pro, or MacBook Air that supports Apple's Multi-Touch trackpad, you can take advantage of two swipe gestures when editing:

- Make a selection in the Event Browser and drag three fingers from bottom to top to add the clip to your movie.

- Swipe three fingers left or right to change the position of a selected clip in the Project Browser.

ORDERING CLIPS

Editing Clips

Remember in Chapter 2 when I advised you to shoot plenty of footage? Take a moment to look back on those lingering, leisurely days, because in this chapter you're going to chop your film into the smallest pieces you can, and still keep it comprehensible. Part of your job as editor is to arrange the many pieces into a unified whole, but you also want to keep your audience awake.

Trimming

In the days of editing film, scenes would be shortened by literally trimming the excess frames with a razor blade. The same idea still applies digitally. Several trimming techniques are available: the Clip Trimmer presents an overview approach, but you can edit more quickly by cropping or deleting selections.

To trim a clip using the Clip Trimmer:

1. In the Project Browser, position the mouse pointer over the clip you want to edit.

2. Click the Action menu and choose Clip Trimmer (**Figure 10.21**); choose Clip Trimmer from the Window menu; double-click the duration indicator; or press Command-R. The Event Browser disappears to make way for the Clip Trimmer.

3. Drag the left and right edges to define the clip's start and end points (**Figure 10.22**). The frames within the yellow selection box remain visible in your movie, while the dimmed areas outside the selection are hidden.

   To preview the selection in the Viewer, click the Play button at the right edge of the Clip Trimmer.

4. Click the Done button when finished. The clip in the Project Browser is made up only of the visible frames.

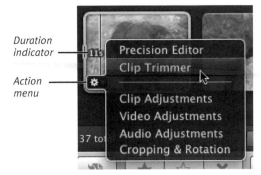

Duration indicator

Action menu

Figure 10.21 Access the Clip Trimmer from the clip's Action menu, or double-click the duration indicator.

Hidden footage

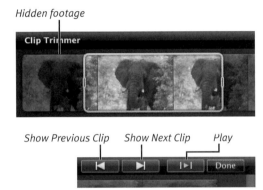

Show Previous Clip   Show Next Clip   Play

Figure 10.22 The Clip Trimmer lets you see an entire clip to better view how the edits apply.

Non-Destructive Editing

In iMovie, clips are *non-destructive*. If you delete a few seconds from the end of a clip, then later decide you need that footage, it's still available to you.

Think of trimming as working with a page of rolled-up blueprints. If you want to view just one portion of the plans, you roll the edges in to hide the rest of the design. In an iMovie video clip, you can hide the frames you choose not to use in your movie. If you need those frames later, you can simply unroll the edges of the clip to display the footage.

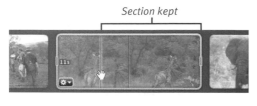

Section kept

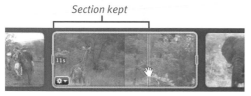

Section kept

Figure 10.23 The position of the playhead depends on which footage is retained when using the Trim to Playhead command.

Selection made

After applying Trim to Selection

Figure 10.24 Cropping removes the footage on either side of the selection.

To trim to the playhead:

1. Position the playhead in the clip you want to edit, keeping in mind that this technique is based on the playhead's proximity to the nearest selection border (**Figure 10.23**):

   ▲ If the playhead is closer to the clip's start point, the footage *after* the playhead remains visible.

   ▲ If the playhead is closer to the clip's end point, the footage *before* the playhead remains visible.

2. Control-click (or right-click) the clip and choose Trim to Playhead from the contextual menu to apply the edit.

To crop a clip:

1. Select part of a clip in the Project Browser.

2. Choose Trim to Selection from the Edit menu, or press Command-B. The selection is retained, and the rest of the clip's frames are deleted (**Figure 10.24**).

✔ Tips

■ For more control when dragging the edges of the selection in the Clip Trimmer, adjust the thumbnail slider to a lower value such as 1/2s (one-half second).

■ To adjust the start and end points in one-frame increments in the Clip Trimmer, place the pointer near the edge you want to edit. Hold the Option key and press the left or right arrow keys; the Viewer displays the first or last visible frame, depending on the edge you're adjusting.

■ In the Clip Trimmer, press the left or right arrow keys to move (slip) the entire selection in one-frame increments.

■ Click any clip in your project, or click Show Previous Clip or Show Next Clip, to edit it without leaving the Clip Trimmer.

EDITING CLIPS

To adjust a trim edit:

1. If you want to recover some of those hidden frames, select a clip and open the Clip Trimmer.

2. Move the start or end point to change the length of the visible clip.

   If you want to change the start *and* end points without altering the clip's duration, click and drag in the middle of the selection to re-center the selection (also known as a slip edit, **Figure 10.25**).

3. Click Done when you're finished editing.

To delete frames from within a clip:

1. Select a portion of a clip.

2. Choose Cut or Delete Selection from the Edit menu, or press the Delete key. The selection is removed, leaving the rest of the footage as two clips (**Figure 10.26**).

   If you choose to cut the selection, it will be stored in the Mac's Clipboard.

Splitting clips

iMovie can also split clips, which lets you break a clip into smaller pieces without deleting (hiding) any of its footage.

To split a clip:

◆ Position the pointer over the frame where you want the split to occur and press Command-Shift-S, or, Control-click to bring up the contextual menu and choose Split Clip.

or

1. Position the pointer over the frame where you want the split to occur and then select to the end of the clip (**Figure 10.27**).

2. Choose Split Clip from the Edit menu. A new clip is created and placed next to the original (**Figure 10.28**).

Selection re-centered

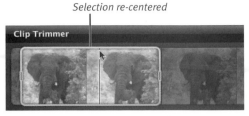

Figure 10.25 Compare the position of this selection with Figure 10.22 to see how the start and end points have changed but not the duration.

Selection made

Previous location of deleted footage

Figure 10.26 When you delete the selected footage, the remaining sections become two clips.

Selection made

Figure 10.27 Splitting a clip requires that you make a selection based on the split point.

Straight corner indicates clip is split.

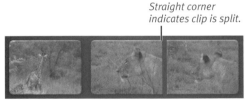

Figure 10.28 A split clip acts like two separate clips, but the corners reveal that the clip has been split.

Copied   *Pasted into middle of clip*

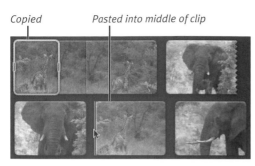

Figure 10.29 After copying a portion of the top-left clip, I pasted it into the middle of the clip in the row below it. Doing so split the second clip.

Figure 10.30 Hold Option and drag to duplicate a clip.

Selecting the middle of a clip

Clip split

Figure 10.31 Splitting a clip from the middle results in three pieces.

Moving Split Clips

As long as the pieces of a split clip remain positioned next to one another, iMovie treats them as split. If you move one segment, the split pieces are considered separate clips. But if you move them back into the proper order, they become split pieces again.

To join split clips:

1. Press Shift and click on any section of the split clip to select it.

2. Choose Join Clip from the Edit menu. The pieces come together again.

Copying and pasting clips

Don't forget the tried-and-true method of copying a clip or some footage and pasting it elsewhere in the filmstrip.

To copy and paste footage:

1. Select a clip or a portion of a clip.

2. Choose Copy from the Edit menu, or press Command-C. The selection is stored in your Mac's Clipboard.

3. Position the Playhead in your movie to the location where you want the clip to appear, then choose Paste from the Edit menu (Command-V). iMovie inserts the new clip at that point, splitting any clip that was present and pushing its remaining footage to the right (**Figure 10.29**).

To duplicate a clip by Option-dragging:

1. Select a clip or a portion of a clip.

2. Option-drag the clip to an empty space in the filmstrip (**Figure 10.30**). Dropping the clip onto another clip brings up the pop-up menu with further options.

✔ Tips

■ After you split a clip or delete a section from its middle, each half still contains all of the frames it had when they were one (thanks to iMovie's non-destructive editing). Use the Clip Trimmer to reveal the hidden frames.

■ If you make a selection in the middle of a clip and then choose Split Clip, the clip is split into three pieces (**Figure 10.31**).

Fine tuning edits

The techniques described thus far are, in general, broad edits designed to chop away unneeded footage in seconds and fractions of seconds. But unless you've set the thumbnail slider way down to 1/2s, it's hard to edit at the frame level. Fine tuning can get you closer to a final edit.

To enable fine tuning:

1. Choose Preferences from the iMovie menu, or press Command-, (comma).

2. Click the Browser icon.

3. Mark the checkbox labeled Show Fine Tuning controls (**Figure 10.32**), and then close the Preferences window. The buttons appear in the lower corners of the clip (**Figure 10.33**).

To apply fine-tune edits (the slow way):

1. Move your pointer over the clip you want to edit and click one of the Fine Tuning buttons, depending on whether you want to edit the start or end of the clip. The clip border becomes orange and the adjoining clip moves out of the way to give you some working room (**Figure 10.34**).

2. Drag the edge handle left or right to hide or restore up to one second of footage (30 frames for NTSC, 25 frames for PAL) (**Figure 10.35**). Keep an eye on the Viewer to see the current frame as you drag.

3. Release the mouse button when you've reached the frame you want.

   To fine tune beyond one second, repeat steps 1 and 2 (or open the clip in the Clip Trimmer or the Precision Editor).

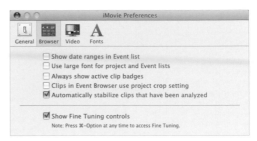

Figure 10.32 The Show Fine Tuning buttons option in preferences makes the controls always visible.

Fine tune start button   *Fine tune end button*

Figure 10.33 The Fine Tuning buttons appear at the bottom edges of each clip.

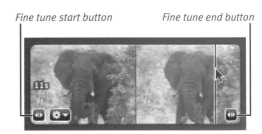

Figure 10.34 Clicking the Fine Tuning button.

This edit is revealing 18 hidden frames and extending the clip to 11.8 seconds.

Figure 10.35 Drag to edit in one-frame increments.

To apply fine-tune edits (the fast way):

◆ Instead of enabling the Fine Tuning buttons at all, simply hold down the Command and Option keys when the pointer is near the edge of a clip. The border turns orange and you can then make a frame-by-frame edit by dragging the edge.

To apply fine-tune edits (the really fast way):

◆ Position the pointer near the edge you want to edit, hold down Option, and press the left or right arrow key.

Get In, Get Out

There are times when long, lingering shots can define a scene or even an entire movie—but not many. When you're editing, concentrate on making your movies *tight*, showing only the essential shots within your scenes. For example, it's a good idea to have an establishing shot of a room, and perhaps a person opening the door. But you don't need to show him closing the door, walking to the center of the room, and beginning a conversation. Jump right to the conversation, since that's probably the core action of the scene. This advice applies to all types of movies: for your trip to the zoo, jump straight to the lions; we don't need to see you bounce along the pathway looking for directions.

Of course, there are always exceptions (*2001: A Space Odyssey* immediately comes to mind), but a tighter film is almost always a better film.

Editing with the Precision Editor

While the Clip Trimmer and Fine Tuning buttons adjust the duration of clips, the Precision Editor focuses on the edit, or the *cut point*, between clips. You can see, in a more visible way, how the clips work together.

There are several ways to open the Precision Editor, which drops down over the Event Library (**Figure 10.36**).

To use the Precision Editor:

◆ Double-click the space between two clips.

◆ Choose Precision Editor from a clip's Action menu. The editor selects the cut point to the left of the clip.

◆ Choose Precision Editor from the Window menu. If a clip is selected, the edit to the left is selected.

◆ Press Command-/ (forward slash). The edit closest to the playhead is selected.

Editing video

The clips in the top row represent footage before the cut point; clips in the bottom row are frames after the cut point. One advantage of the Precision Editor is that you can view an entire clip's worth of footage, as you can in the Clip Trimmer, while also seeing surrounding clips; dimmed sections are hidden.

You can adjust the position of the cut point in several ways.

To edit the cut point:

◆ Click once within a clip to establish the cut point (**Figure 10.37**). iMovie shifts the position of the clip relative to the other clip to position the cut point at that spot.

Edit selected   Precision Editor   Cut point

Figure 10.36 The Precision Editor.

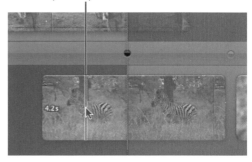

Click to adjust cut point.

After edit

Figure 10.37 Clicking moves the cut point in the clip.

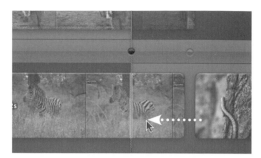

Figure 10.38 Drag the thumbstrip left or right to change the location of the cut point.

Figure 10.39 When you drag the cut point in the top clip, the position of the point in the bottom clip remains unchanged. In this case, the entire thumbstrip moves with the cut point as you drag.

Figure 10.40 Compare the position of the cut point in the bottom clip, when dragging the middle point, to the position in Figure 10.39. The movie's duration doesn't change, but the visible frames of both clips do.

◆ Drag one of the clips until the cut point is at the frame you want (**Figure 10.38**). The Viewer displays the frame below the cut point, not the frame under the pointer.

◆ Drag the cut point itself. Three options are available, which create different results:

  ▲ Drag the cut point in the top clip to modify that clip's cut point but keep the frame in the bottom clip (**Figure 10.39**). The duration of the top clip changes.

  ▲ Drag the cut point in the bottom clip to modify that clip's cut point but keep the frame in the top clip. The duration of the bottom clip changes.

  ▲ Drag the cut point at the middle point between the two clips (**Figure 10.40**). The duration of both clips (and the entire movie) remains the same.

✔ Tips

■ For more accurate editing, enable the Display Time as HH:MM:SS:Frames option (timecode) in iMovie's preferences.

■ Click the Play button to preview three seconds around the cut point.

■ The Precision Editor is the best place to edit transitions. See Chapter 13 for specifics on how to do it.

■ Repositioning the middle of the cut point performs what's more commonly known as a "roll edit" in video editing circles.

■ Set the Viewer to its Small size (press Command-8) to maximize the size of the Precision Editor.

■ Click the circle icons in the middle bar to jump to other edit points. You can also click the space between clips in the Project Browser without exiting the Precision Editor.

EDITING WITH THE PRECISION EDITOR

Offsetting audio

Here's another benefit to working in the Precision Editor: you can offset the cut point of a video clip's audio without working with it as a separate audio clip (see Chapter 12 for more on working with audio clips). This capability enables you to overlay the audio from one clip onto the other.

To offset audio:

1. In the Precision Editor, click the Show or Hide Audio Tracks button to view the audio waveforms (**Figure 10.41**).

2. Drag the cut point in an audio track to change the point at which the audio begins (**Figure 10.42**).

   To reposition the cut point in both clips simultaneously and prevent overlap of both clips' audio, hold Shift and drag.

Editing extra elements

The Precision Editor is focused on working with video clips and transitions, but you can also view and edit other iMovie elements such as cutaways, titles, and music tracks.

To view and edit extras:

1. In the Precision Editor, click the Show or Hide Extras button to display other elements (**Figure 10.43**).

2. For many items, such as titles and audio tracks, drag their edges to change their durations.

To exit the Precision Editor:

◆ Click the Done button, or press Esc, Return, or Enter.

✔ Tip

■ Clicking a clip in the Project Browser switches the Precision Editor to the Clip Trimmer. Click an edit point to return.

Audio waveform   *Show or Hide Audio Tracks*

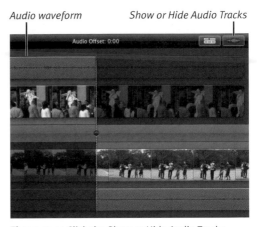

Figure 10.41 Click the Show or Hide Audio Tracks button to display audio waveforms.

Audio cut point

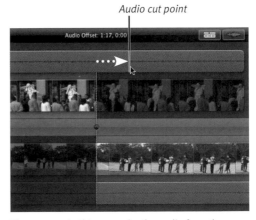

Figure 10.42 In this example, the audio from the preceding clip (at top) will continue to play during the first 1:17 of the following clip (at bottom).

Cutaway clip   *Title*   *Show or Hide Extras*

Figure 10.43 View other objects in the Precision Editor, such as titles and cutaways.

Comment Marker

Figure 10.44 Drag a comment marker to your movie so you can jump back to that spot later.

Figure 10.45 Give your marker a name to locate it easily.

Figure 10.46 The (nearly invisible) pop-up menu near the marker icons lets you jump to those spots.

Figure 10.47 Look for the arrow that indicates a chapter marker.

Using Comment Markers

When editing long movies, it's sometimes difficult to locate a particular scene without skimming through the movie in the Project Browser. iMovie's comment markers let you set placeholders that are easy to locate. The markers don't appear in your final movie in any way—they exist purely for your organizational pleasure. (For information on *chapter markers*, which are used to create chapters for iDVD, see Chapter 18.)

To set a comment marker:

1. Make sure Show Advanced Tools is enabled in iMovie's preferences.

2. Click the Comment Marker icon and drag it to a frame in your project (**Figure 10.44**).

   You can also Control-click (or right-click) a frame and choose Add Comment Marker from the contextual menu.

3. Enter a name for the marker and press Return (**Figure 10.45**).

To relocate a comment marker:

◆ Click and drag the marker elsewhere in the movie project.

To delete a comment marker:

◆ Select the marker and press Delete.

To jump to a comment marker:

◆ Click the triangle to the right of the marker icons and choose from the pop-up menu that appears (**Figure 10.46**).

✔ Tip

■ Comment markers and chapter markers look awfully similar: one is brown and one is a rust color. However, chapter markers also include an arrow before the name for easier identification (**Figure 10.47**).

Changing Clip Speed

Creating sped-up or slow-motion imagery previously involved changing a camera's shutter speed (the faster the film moved, the more individual pictures could be shot, creating slow motion, for example). In iMovie, all you have to do is move a slider. You can also reverse the clip's direction.

To speed up or slow down video:

1. Double-click the clip you wish to alter. You can also select it and click the Inspector button in the toolbar, or press the I key. The Inspector appears with the Clip Adjustments panel active.

2. Move the Speed slider toward the rabbit (faster) or the turtle (slower) to change the speed (**Figure 10.48**).

3. Click Done.

To reverse video playback:

◆ In the Clip Adjustments inspector, enable the Direction: Reverse checkbox.

✔ Tips

■ Some movie formats need to be converted before you can change the clip speed. Click the Convert Entire Clip button to enable the feature (**Figure 10.49**).

■ You can also enter a value into the text field to the right of the slider. You're not limited to the tick mark values on the slider, so you can set the speed to be 118% of normal if you want. The field below that tells you the clip's changed duration. But you can also exceed the boundaries of the speed slider. Enter any number between 5% and 2000%.

■ The audio in speed-adjusted clips is similarly slowed, accelerated, or reversed. Consider making the clip silent and playing some other audio track in its place.

Speed slider

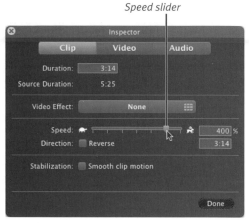

Figure 10.48 Speed up or slow down your clip in the Clip Adjustments panel of the Inspector.

Figure 10.49 Some formats require a conversion step before you can change the clip speed.

■ You can also simply click a portion of the slider's scale to adjust the speed, instead of moving the slider knob.

■ Changing clip speed is especially helpful on clips of scenery or backgrounds. Draw out scenes you shot too quickly, or speed up long pans to improve pacing.

■ A bug in iMovie '09 can render some clips mute if any clip in your project uses a custom speed value (i.e., not the tick marks provided). Hopefully a fix is available by the time you read this tip.

Clip from Project Browser

Clip from Event Browser

Figure 10.50 The stabilization option differs between clips in an Event and in your project before analysis.

Viewing the Inspector's Clip Adjustments Panel

Many editing operations occur in the Clip Adjustments panel of the Inspector, and there are what seem to be an equal number of ways to access that floating window. The easiest method is to double-click a clip, which is what I'll refer to most of the time. However, the following actions also make it appear, arranged in order of how likely I am to use it:

◆ Press the I key.

◆ Click the Inspector button on the toolbar. The Clip Adjustments panel appears by default.

◆ Choose Clip Adjustments from a clip's Action menu.

◆ Choose Clip Adjustments from the Window menu.

Stabilizing Shaky Video

The mark of a homemade movie is usually the shakiness of the picture: lightweight handheld cameras tend to bounce unless you've locked them down on a tripod. With iMovie's image stabilization feature, you can smooth the bumps in your movie.

Image stabilization works in two steps. First, the video is analyzed, during which iMovie determines how much each frame should be zoomed and rotated to remove excessive motion based on the previous frame. This analysis can happen when you import the footage (see Chapter 8), or on a clip-by-clip basis. Then, when you add an analyzed clip to your movie, you set the amount of stabilization to apply.

To analyze clips for stabilization:

1. In the Event Browser or the Project Browser, double-click a clip to bring up the Inspector.

2. For clips in the Project Browser, enable the Stabilization: Smooth Clip Motion checkbox (**Figure 10.50**).

   For clips in the Event Browser, click the Analyze Entire Clip button.

   Depending on the duration of the clips, analysis can take some time, anywhere from four to eight times the length of the footage.

✔ Tip

■ iMovie's stabilization analysis takes up very little disk space, because it's keeping track only of the changes to the frames, not rendering new footage. So if you have the time to analyze everything at import, that's the least intrusive option for when you're in the middle of editing.

To apply image stabilization:

1. Double-click a clip in the Project Browser to bring up the Clip Adjustments panel of the Inspector.

2. Click the Smooth clip motion checkbox to apply the stabilization.

   iMovie sets the Maximum Zoom slider to what it thinks is a good level of stabilization (**Figure 10.51**). However, feel free to experiment with the setting; sometimes a slightly shaky picture is better than one that looks artificial from the effect.

   (By the way, the slider is labeled Maximum Zoom because iMovie zooms further into the image to compensate for shakiness, as shown in **Figure 10.52**.)

To hide footage with excessive shake:

◆ Frames that are too shaky to benefit from iMovie's image stabilization are indicated by a red squiggly line. Click the button with a similar icon below the Event Library to hide those frames (**Figure 10.53**).

✔ Tips

■ The percentage value in the Maximum Zoom slider is based on the entire clip. If you edit out a section with a lot of motion, the clip may not require as much zoom.

■ Some footage, especially if it was shot using a camera with a CMOS sensor (see Chapter 1) can exhibit a "heat wave" effect if too much stabilization is applied.

■ Standard-definition video can appear slightly blurry when stabilized, since iMovie is zooming in on the footage.

■ Clips with image stabilization applied display a hand badge (). An orange or red badge indicates some areas of the stabilized clip are excessively shaky.

Maximum Zoom slider

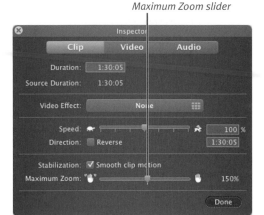

Figure 10.51 The Maximum Zoom slider controls the amount of image stabilization.

None

Maximum

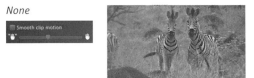

Figure 10.52 The more zoom applied to a clip, the more stable the motion appears. Note that the zebra on the far left has been cropped out of the frame with maximum zoom applied. (To view this example video, go to jeffcarlson.com/imovie/stabilize.mov.)

Figure 10.53 Footage with too much shake is marked with a squiggly red line. Click the similar-looking button to hide those frames.

Position playhead

Figure 10.54 After clicking the Crop button, you can position the play-head, where it remains in place.

Figure 10.55 iMovie crops the widescreen clip so that the image fills the project's aspect ratio.

Figure 10.56 The crop region has been resized and moved to focus on a specific area of the video.

Cropping and Rotating

The downside to iMovie's capability to mix and match formats and aspect ratios is making them play nice in the same frame. Importing widescreen footage into a standard DV project, for example, results in black bars above and below the image to occupy the unused space (called *letterboxing*).

iMovie gives you the option of cropping footage to use the entire screen (or even eliminate a portion of a scene) or of fitting the entire clip into the frame with black bars.

To crop a clip:

1. Select a clip and click the Crop button in the toolbar, or press C. The clip's thumbnail displays a thin yellow border and a circle within the playhead (**Figure 10.54**); position the playhead and it will stick (skimming is turned off).

2. In the Viewer, click the Crop button. iMovie displays a highlighted region that matches the project's aspect ratio (**Figure 10.55**).

3. To reposition the cropping region, click within it and drag. To change the size of the region, drag a corner handle; the aspect ratio remains consistent. You can resize the region down to 50 percent of the original size (**Figure 10.56**).

4. Click the Play button to preview the cropped clip in the Viewer. Click Done when you're finished editing.

✔ Tip

■ Resizing a crop region decreases the video resolution. If you're starting with high-def footage you may not notice, but resizing standard DV can get fuzzy.

To fit a clip:

1. Choose a clip and press C to view the crop controls.

2. In the Viewer, click the Fit button. The video appears with black bars to fill out the project's aspect ratio.

   If you've previously applied a crop, click the Fit button to revert to the clip's original aspect ratio.

3. Click Done when you're finished.

Rotating clips

In Chapter 2, I mentioned that some people use a camcorder like a still camera and rotate it to take vertical shots. If you find yourself with scenes like that, or you want to just rotate your video for your own entertainment, here's how to do it.

To rotate a clip:

1. Choose a clip and press C.

2. Click one of the rotation buttons to rotate the clip 90 degrees clockwise or counter-clockwise (**Figure 10.57**). Because the rotated clip won't match the project's aspect ratio, iMovie applies a crop.

   If you prefer to view the entire image with black bars on the sides, click the Fit button (**Figure 10.58**).

3. Click Done when you're finished. The rotated clip looks like you shot it that way (**Figure 10.59**).

✔ Tips

- Specify whether clips are automatically cropped or sized to fit. Choose Project Properties from the File menu, click the Timing button, and change the Initial Video Placement setting.

- When cropping a clip, click other clips to apply cropping without clicking Done.

Rotate counter-clockwise   Rotate clockwise

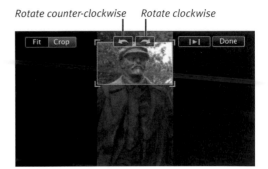

Figure 10.57 Rotate video in 90-degree increments.

Figure 10.58 To account for the change in aspect ratio, you may want to crop the rotated image.

Figure 10.59 After you've rotated and cropped the clip, it fills the entire screen when played back.

Video Effect button

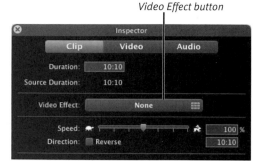

Figure 10.60 The name of the current effect appears in the Video Effect button.

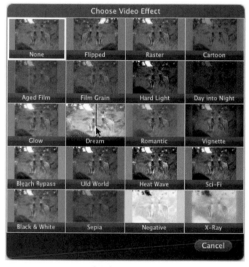

Figure 10.61 Skim across each box to preview the entire clip with that effect in the Viewer.

Effect applied

Figure 10.62 This icon tells you an effect is applied to the clip.

Applying Video Effects

Go watch five movies in the theater and you'll probably see five different visual textures—they may all be in color (or might not), but the "looks" are likely to be quite divergent. Straight-ahead color video isn't always what you're looking for. iMovie includes several visual filters you can apply to your footage, such as aged film or a reversed x-ray appearance.

To apply a video effect:

1. Double-click a clip in the Project Browser to bring up the Clip Adjustments panel in the Inspector (**Figure 10.60**).

2. Click the Video Effect button. The Choose Video Effect dialog appears with a grid of available effects (**Figure 10.61**).

3. Skim over each effect to preview the clip with that appearance in the viewer. When you've decided which one to use, click it.

4. Click Done to dismiss the Inspector.

✔ Tips

- A clip's thumbnail icon in the Project Browser doesn't display the effect you've applied. Instead, look for an "i" badge to note an effect is applied (**Figure 10.62**).

- Unfortunately, you can apply only one effect to a clip. However, there is a little wiggle room: you can combine an effect plus a video adjustment. So, for example, if you want aged film that looks black and white, apply the Aged Film effect here and then reduce the Saturation to zero (see the next page).

APPLYING VIDEO EFFECTS

Making Video Adjustments

The best thing you can do to improve the quality of your video is to shoot good-quality footage. And while that's a noble goal, it's just not always possible—your camera didn't adjust its white point correctly, the day was too cloudy, you forgot to hire a director of photography for your multimillion-dollar major studio picture....

As you might expect, iMovie's adjustments aren't nearly up to the same quality as the tools found in Final Cut Studio, but they can be pretty useful for tweaking color or lightening a dark scene.

To adjust color:

1. Double-click the clip you want to edit and click the Video button; select the clip and click the Video Adjustments button in the toolbar; or, select the clip and press V.

2. Use any of the following controls (**Figure 10.63**) to change the look of the footage previewed in the Viewer.
   - ▲ **Auto.** Click this button to let iMovie calculate the best settings.
   - ▲ **Levels.** The histogram at the top of the window represents the levels of red, blue, and green in the current frame. The sliders below the graph represent the darkest and lightest values (pure black or white).

     Drag the left slider toward the middle to darken the image; drag the right slider similarly to lighten the image. Doing so treats the furthermost colors on the outside edges as darkest or lightest (**Figure 10.64**).
   - ▲ **Exposure.** This slider brightens or darkens the video's highlights.
   - ▲ **Brightness.** This slider controls the overall lightness of the clip.

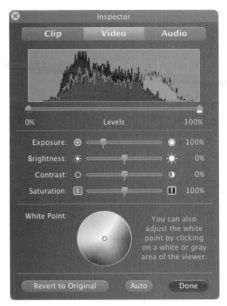

Figure 10.63 A selection of color enhancement tools are available to adjust your video.

Figure 10.64 The levels in the original video (left) are fairly well balanced. Drastically moving the white level slider brightens the image far too much (right).

Figure 10.65 The White Point setting often warms up cloudy day footage that would otherwise be drab.

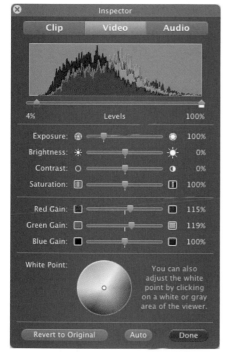

Figure 10.66 iMovie's advanced mode adds color gain sliders to the Video Adjustments panel of the Inspector.

▲ **Contrast.** Accentuate the differences between light and dark.

▲ **Saturation.** Drag this slider to change the color intensity.

▲ **White Point.** This control tells iMovie which color value equals white; the rest of the colors are based on that value. Move the point within the color wheel to adjust the white point, which can also affect the clip's color cast (**Figure 10.65**). Or, click within the Viewer to specify which color should be treated as white (it also bases its settings on gray values).

▲ **Revert to Original.** If you don't like the adjustments you made, click here to go back to the original settings.

3. When you're finished making adjustments, click the Done button.

To manipulate red, green, and blue colors (advanced mode):

1. In iMovie's preferences, enable Show Advanced Tools.

2. Bring up the Video Adjustments panel of the Inspector (**Figure 10.66**).

3. Move the Red Gain, Green Gain, and Blue Gain sliders to adjust those colors.

✔ Tips

■ Video adjustments can be applied to clips in both the Project Browser and the Event Library.

■ Clips with video adjustments applied display a special badge (⊙). Double-clicking that badge brings up the Video Adjustments panel.

■ Remember that you can do some serious damage to your image—and I mean that in a good way. Crank the sliders when a scene calls for odd visuals. The original remains untouched on your hard disk.

MAKING VIDEO ADJUSTMENTS

Creating a Cutaway

A cutaway is a common editing technique where a new image appears over the top of existing audio, such as showing a shot of someone reacting to what's happening in the main clip. Cutaways are also often used to cover glitches that invariably crop up, such as bumping the camera, losing focus, or having someone unexpectedly walk into the frame.

Once added, a cutaway clip can be edited like a regular clip: trim it, apply video effects, change its audio, etc. You can change its opacity to reveal the underlying clip, too.

The cutaway feature also opens the door to adding masks, watermarks, and other overlays.

To create a cutaway:

1. Make sure the Show Advanced Tools option is enabled in iMovie's preferences.

2. Drag a selection onto a clip in your project (**Figure 10.67**).

3. Choose Cutaway from the pop-up menu (**Figure 10.68**).

   The clip is added on top of the base clip; the shaded area below it indicates that the base clip is hidden during the cutaway, even though the base clip's audio continues to be heard (**Figure 10.69**).

To edit a cutaway:

◆ Trim the cutaway clip's duration by dragging its edge handles or opening it in the Clip Trimmer.

◆ Drag the cutaway left or right to reposition it above the base clip.

Figure 10.67 Drag what will be the cutaway clip onto the top of a clip in your project.

Figure 10.68 Choose Cutaway from the pop-up menu.

Figure 10.69 The cutaway clip hides the image, but not the audio, of the base clip.

Figure 10.70 Cutaway clips gain two additional options in the Clip Adjustments panel of the Inspector.

CREATING A CUTAWAY

Figure 10.71 The Opacity slider in the Inspector makes the cutaway transparent.

Figure 10.72 I created an image on a transparent background in Photoshop.

Figure 10.73
The image appears as a cutaway in the Project Browser. The completed effect can be seen in the Viewer (below).

◆ Double-click the clip to open the Inspector and use the tools there. Two new options appear for cutaway clips (**Figure 10.70**):

  ▲ Click to enable a manual cutaway fade (a cross-dissolve between the base clip and the cutaway) and use the slider to set the duration; the fade applies at both ends of the clip.

  ▲ Drag the Opacity slider to change the transparency of the cutaway clip (**Figure 10.71**).

To create an overlay using a cutaway:

1. In an image editor such as Adobe Photoshop, create an image matching the dimensions of your project (**Figure 10.72**). Make sure it's on a separate layer to give it transparency.

2. Save the image as a PNG file with transparency enabled.

3. Drag the image file from the Finder to your project and choose Cutaway from the pop-up menu that appears (**Figure 10.73**).

✔ Tips

■ You can't perform Insert or Replace edits on a cutaway, so if you want to change the cutaway to another clip, you must add it separately.

■ You may wish to mute the cutaway's audio if it's distracting, or alternately set it so the base clip ducks while the cutaway is playing (see Chapter 12).

Creating a Picture in Picture Effect

Similar to a cutaway, iMovie's picture in picture effect places a clip over the top of another clip, but instead of occupying the entire frame, the second clip appears in a resizable rectangle.

To create a picture in picture effect:

1. Make sure the Show Advanced Tools option is enabled in iMovie's preferences.

2. Drag a clip onto another clip in the Project Browser.

3. Choose Picture in Picture from the pop-up menu (**Figure 10.74**). The clip is added on top of the base clip. You can see the effect in the Viewer.

To edit a picture in picture effect:

◆ With the picture in picture clip selected in the Project Browser, go to the Viewer and drag the handles of the added clip (**Figure 10.75**).

◆ Drag the center of the clip in the Viewer to reposition it within the frame.

◆ Double-click the clip in the Viewer or the Project Browser to open the Clip Adjustments panel of the Inspector, where you can edit the following options (**Figure 10.76**):

   ▲ The PIP Effect controls how the new picture appears and goes away: Dissolve fades the image in and out; Zoom expands and contracts from a single point; and Swap fills the entire frame with the added clip and makes the original clip appear in the picture in picture box.

   ▲ The Border Width, Border Color, and Drop Shadow options style the picture in picture box (**Figure 10.77**).

Figure 10.74 Choose Picture in Picture from the pop-up menu.

Figure 10.75 Change the size and position of the picture in picture effect within the Viewer.

Figure 10.76 These options can make the picture in picture image more visible.

Figure 10.77 The box here has a thick white border with a drop shadow applied.

Figure 10.78 A bright green felt cloth makes a great green screen. I've deliberately introduced some problem areas for this example: the left edge and the rounded fold to the right.

Figure 10.79 Choose Green Screen from the pop-up menu to add the effect.

Figure 10.80 iMovie has done a pretty good job of removing the green background, except for the problem areas.

Creating a Green Screen Effect

Today's special-effects–heavy movies make extensive use of green screens to swap in any footage behind the main action. That plucky band of space adventurers may appear to be looking out into the black of space, but really they're staring at a bright green wall. The other spaceships and starfields are added later. Using iMovie and $10 worth of fabric, you can accomplish the same thing.

To shoot green screen footage:

◆ You don't need a specific color of green in your background; iMovie looks for all shades of the color green (**Figure 10.78**). (It must be green, though. You can't specify another color.) Your best bet is to find a bright green that doesn't normally appear in most scenes.

◆ Make sure the green fills the background (although iMovie can compensate a little for non-green areas).

◆ Set up the lighting so that there are no shadows projected onto the green screen.

◆ Don't include green objects or clothing.

◆ Avoid reflective materials that could pick up some of the surrounding green; they'll become partially transparent.

To create a green screen effect:

1. Make sure the Show Advanced Tools option is enabled in iMovie's preferences.

2. Drag a clip onto another clip in the Project Browser.

3. Choose Green Screen from the pop-up menu (**Figure 10.79**). The clip is added on top of the base clip and the effect appears in the Viewer (**Figure 10.80**).

To improve the green screen effect:

1. Select the green screen clip in the Project Browser.

2. In the Viewer, click the Cropped button. iMovie displays a four-cornered shape that acts as a "garbage matte."

3. Drag the corner handles to define the active area of the green screen clip (**Figure 10.81**). iMovie makes everything outside the matte transparent, whether or not it's green.

4. Click Done to apply the effect (**Figure 10.82**).

✔ Tips

- When cropping the green screen clip, make sure the matte takes into account the movement of the clip's subject (**Figure 10.83**).

- When shooting, capture a second or two of the green screen background with nothing else in the frame. Then, in iMovie, double-click the green screen clip to bring up the Inspector and try enabling the Background: Subtract Last Frame checkbox. iMovie uses that as a reference for which areas to crop out.

- You can't apply a transition to a green screen clip.

Figure 10.81 Specify the important area of your clip.

Figure 10.82 The finished clip no longer shows the problem areas.

Figure 10.83 Cropping too tightly can lead to an odd sliced-off image, as with the right edge here.

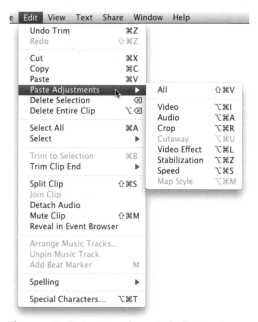

Figure 10.84 Once you apply a set of adjustments, you can paste them to other clips and save yourself some repetitive work.

Figure 10.85 This clip has a Black and White video effect applied, but its thumbnail still appears in color in the Project Browser.

Copying and Pasting Adjustments

When you make adjustments, the settings are applied to the entire clip. If other clips in your movie were shot at the same time (or you just want the same adjustments), you can apply the same settings without having to duplicate them one by one.

To copy and paste adjustments:

1. Select a clip that has adjustments applied.

2. Choose Copy from the Edit menu or from the contextual menu, or press Command-C.

3. Select the clip (or clips) to which you want to apply the adjustments.

4. Go to the Edit menu, highlight the Paste Adjustments submenu, and choose which adjustments to apply (**Figure 10.84**).

✔ Tip

- Filmstrip thumbnails don't display video adjustments—for example, a black and white clip still appears in color in the browsers (**Figure 10.85**). Skim over the clip to see how it appears in the Viewer.

Working with Source Clips

It's not uncommon for me to chop up a single long clip into so many little pieces that I've lost track of where they are. Trimming lets you cobble together pieces, but what if you want to just start fresh?

Thanks to the way iMovie stores files, you can recover a pristine version of a clip. Clips you create don't actually exist as new files on your hard disk. Instead, iMovie simply notes what changes have been applied to clips, and grabs the necessary information from the clip's original data file.

To revert a clip:

1. Select a clip in the Project Browser that you want to restore.

2. Control-click to bring up the contextual menu and choose Reveal in Event Browser (**Figure 10.86**). The segment you selected appears highlighted in gray on the source clip.

3. Grab the footage you want from the source clip.

To locate a source file on disk:

1. In either the Project Browser or Event Browser, select a clip and bring up the contextual menu (Control-click).

2. Choose Reveal in Finder. A new Finder window appears with the clip selected (**Figure 10.87**).

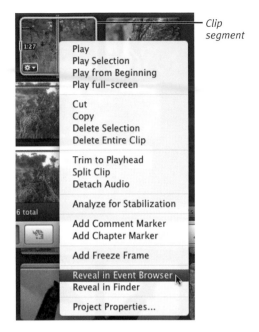

Clip segment

Source clip with segment selected

Figure 10.86 Choose Reveal in Event Browser to locate a clip's source.

Figure 10.87 The Finder's Cover Flow view provides easy previews of your source files.

EDITING
STILL PICTURES

After purchasing a camcorder, I didn't throw away my trusty digital still camera. In fact, on a day-to-day basis, I find myself taking more photos than shooting video footage; compact digital cameras are just so easy to carry around.

iMovie makes it easy to incorporate those stills into your movie projects, whether you're creating a slideshow, adding a series of pictures to accentuate video footage, or creating graphics or Photoshop-enhanced title screens. With iMovie, it's a snap to add any image from your iPhoto library.

This chapter also includes information about the highly touted Ken Burns Effect, a pan-and-zoom operation that adds motion to otherwise static images.

Importing Photos

You can easily import photos you've scanned or taken with a digital still camera. iMovie makes this process easier by giving you access to your library of pictures in iPhoto (as well as Aperture and Photo Booth).

To locate photos using the Photos Browser:

1. Display the Photos Browser by choosing Photos from the Window menu, clicking the Photos button in the toolbar, or pressing Command-2.

2. Click a photo source, such as iPhoto, in the top pane (**Figure 11.1**). Your photo library is shown in the preview area.

3. Use any of the following tools to locate photos to import:

   ▲ If you want to access a specific photo album, choose its name from the list. You can also choose Events and browse iPhoto Events by skimming the mouse pointer over them. Double-click an Event to view the photos contained within it.

   ▲ Type a name into the search field to locate pictures based on their titles (**Figure 11.2**). Clicking the magnifying glass icon reveals options to search by keyword or rating.

   ▲ Select an Event in the Event Library that contains footage in your movie. Then, in the Photos Browser, click the Show photos checkbox and choose a date range from the pop-up menu (**Figure 11.3**).

✔ Tip

■ Click the divider between the source list and the photos and drag up; the list becomes a single pop-up menu and makes more room for images (**Figure 11.4**).

Click other sources in the list.   *Photos button*

Figure 11.1 All the pictures in your iPhoto library are accessible from within the Photos Browser.

Change thumbnail size

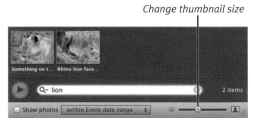

Figure 11.2 Use the search field to quickly locate photos using names you assigned them in iPhoto.

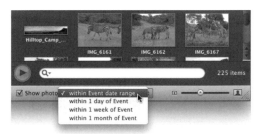

Figure 11.3 Figuring that you shot still photos and video at the same time, iMovie can display pictures taken in the same date range of a video Event.

Figure 11.4 The photo sources as a pop-up menu.

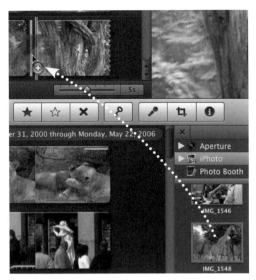

Figure 11.5 Drag a picture from the Photos Browser to the Project Browser to add it to your movie.

Figure 11.6 Still photos can take advantage of video edits and effects when you drop them onto clips.

Figure 11.7 Add a folder from the Finder to easily access its photos from within iMovie.

To import pictures from iPhoto:

◆ Drag the picture from the Photos Browser to a space between clips in the Project Browser (**Figure 11.5**).

or

1. Drag the picture *onto* a clip in the Project Browser.

2. From the pop-up menu that appears, choose an action (**Figure 11.6**):

   ▲ Replace removes the existing clip and adds the new photo, which inherits the same duration as the prior clip.

   ▲ Insert splits the existing clip at the playhead and adds the photo at that point; the photo has the default duration (four seconds, unless specified differently in the Project Properties dialog; more about that on the next page).

   ▲ Cutaway, Picture in Picture, and Green Screen apply those effects using the photo; see Chapter 10 for details.

   The Ken Burns Effect is automatically applied to the photo when it's imported, but you can edit or turn off the effect, as discussed later in this chapter.

To import photos from another source:

◆ Drag an image file from the Finder to iMovie's Project Browser.

◆ If you'll be importing many photos from the Finder, drag the folder they're in to the top pane of the Photos Browser. A new Folders folder is created, and its contents are accessible from the browser (**Figure 11.7**).

✔ Tip

■ Double-clicking a photo thumbnail in the Photos Browser expands it to fit within the preview area for a better view.

Adding Motion with the Ken Burns Effect

Who says still photos must remain still? A common effect used by documentary film-makers is *pan and zoom*, where the camera moves across a still image, zooms in on (or out of) a portion of the image, or performs a combination of the two.

To change whether the Ken Burns Effect is automatically applied:

1. Choose Project Properties from the File menu or press Command-J.

2. Click the Timing button.

3. From the Initial Video Placement pop-up menu (**Figure 11.8**), choose one of the following:

   ▲ **Fit in Frame.** iMovie includes the entire photo, possibly resulting in black bars at the edges to account for the difference in aspect ratios between the photo and project.

   ▲ **Crop.** The photo fills the frame.

   ▲ **Ken Burns.** A basic Ken Burns Effect is applied to every new photo added to the project.

4. Click OK to apply the setting, which affects new photos you add (not stills you've already imported).

To edit the Ken Burns Effect:

1. Add a photo to your project. If the Ken Burns Effect was automatically applied, skip to Step 4.

2. Click the photo's Crop icon or press C, which loads the image into the Viewer.

3. Click the Ken Burns button. iMovie applies a basic zoom effect (**Figure 11.9**).

4. Position the effect's starting frame: click the green Start rectangle and move and

Figure 11.8 Specify how new photos are treated.

Figure 11.9 Ken Burns Effect is applied.

Figure 11.10 The Start frame has been cropped and shifted to the left to accentuate this giraffe's head. The yellow arrow indicates the direction the zoom effect will follow when played back.

Figure 11.11 Now we're setting up the last frame of the effect—zoomed in and shifted to the right.

Start

End

Figure 11.12 The completed Ken Burns Effect zooms out and pans to view all the giraffes.

Reverse button

Figure 11.13 Click the Reverse button to quickly swap the Start and Finish settings.

Ken Who?

Ever one to capitalize on name recognition, Apple named this feature after Ken Burns, a documentary filmmaker who frequently employs the effect in his popular documentaries. Examples include *The Civil War, JAZZ,* and *Baseball.* For more information, see www.pbs.org/kenburns/.

resize it (**Figure 11.10**). When played back, the contents of the Start rectangle will fill the window; press the Play button to preview the effect.

5. Set the final frame of the effect by clicking the red End box to select it and then resizing and positioning it (**Figure 11.11**).

6. When the effect is set up to your liking, click Done.

Figure 11.12 approximates the effect as it appears when played back.

To apply the same effect to multiple still photos:

1. After configuring the Ken Burns Effect on one photo, select the clip and choose Copy from the Edit menu to copy its attributes.

2. Select another still photo.

3. Go to the Edit menu and choose Crop from the Paste Adjustments submenu (or press Command-Option-R). The effect is applied.

4. Repeat Steps 2 and 3 for any other photos.

✔ Tips

■ If you decide you want your effect to run backwards from the way you set it, click the Reverse button to swap the Start and End settings (**Figure 11.13**).

■ The speed of the effect depends on the duration of the clip. For a slower effect, increase the photo's duration.

■ Back-to-back photos with Ken Burns applied alternate the direction of the motion. So, if one clip zooms in, the next will automatically zoom out when added.

■ For much more control over pan-and-zoom effects, try Photo to Movie (lqgraphics.com/software/).

ADDING MOTION WITH THE KEN BURNS EFFECT

The Ken Burns Effect has a surprising limitation when working with vertically-oriented photos. The boundaries of the Start and End frames don't extend beyond the image, which means you can't view an entire vertical clip (**Figure 11.14**)—without some finessing beforehand, that is.

To fit an entire image in a Ken Burns Effect:

1. In a program such as Adobe Photoshop Elements, open the vertical photo you want to edit. I'm using Photoshop Elements as the example here because it offers the capability to resize the image canvas, which is different than resizing the image, a feature included with most image editors.

2. Go to the Canvas Size (or similar) dialog (**Figure 11.15**).

3. Change the Width value using the following formulas:

   ▲ For a project with a Standard (4:3) aspect ratio, multiply the height by 1.333 and enter that result in the Width field.

   ▲ For a project with a Widescreen (16:9) aspect ratio, multiply the height by 1.777 and enter that result in the Width field.

4. Apple the change, and then save the image in JPEG format.

5. Drag the image file from the Finder to iMovie's Project Browser and apply the Ken Burns Effect (**Figure 11.16**).

Figure 11.14 The Start and End frames are limited to the photo's edges, so you can't see the entire image.

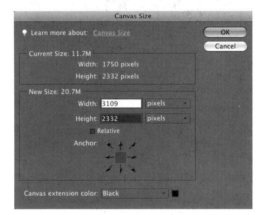

Figure 11.15 Photoshop Elements for Mac includes the capability to resize the canvas surrounding the photo.

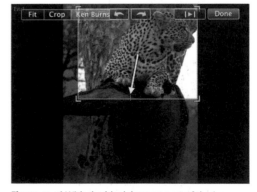

Figure 11.16 With the black bars as part of the image, you can zoom out to view the photo top to bottom.

Figure 11.17 Open the Clip Adjustments panel of the Inspector to edit a still clip's duration.

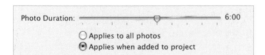

Figure 11.18 The duration of still photos can be applied to just one image or to all photos in the project.

Figure 11.19 Set a default duration in the Project Properties dialog.

Changing the Duration of a Still Clip

Although a still clip appears in the filmstrip like any other video clip, iMovie treats it slightly differently. Instead of trimming a photo, you simply change its duration. You can also set a default duration for incoming photos or all photos in a project.

To change a picture's duration:

1. Choose Clip Adjustments from the Action menu (**Figure 11.17**). You can also choose Clip Adjustments from the Window menu or the contextual menu, or press the I key.

2. In the Inspector, enter a new value into the Duration field (**Figure 11.18**).

3. To set the new duration to all photos in the project, mark the Applies to all stills checkbox. Click Done.

To set a default photo duration:

1. Choose Project Properties from the File menu or press Command-J.

2. In the dialog that appears, move the Photo Duration slider to set a new default time (**Figure 11.19**).

3. Choose when the duration should apply: either to all photos currently in the project, or when a photo is added. Click OK.

✔ Tips

- When you change a photo's duration, the Ken Burns Effect adapts to the new length.

- With the Inspector visible, you can apply a video effect or make adjustments to the image in the Video Adjustments panel (see Chapter 10).

Creating a Freeze Frame

Thousands of still images flicker by as we're watching video—sometimes too quickly. Perhaps you'd like to linger on a sunset or highlight the one brief moment when everyone in your family was looking at the camera. You can create a still photo from a single frame of video.

To create a freeze frame:

1. Position the playhead at the frame you wish to use.

2. Hold Control and click to bring up the contextual menu, and then choose Add Freeze Frame (**Figure 11.20**). A new still photo clip is added at the playhead and given the duration specified in the Project Properties dialog (**Figure 11.21**).

✔ Tips

■ Once the still has been created, it's treated like any other still photo, which means you can set up a Ken Burns Effect for it.

■ Remember that you're still working in video resolution, so your freeze frame won't be the same high-quality that you'd get by taking a photo using a digital still camera.

■ To grab that still photo and use it somewhere else (such as adding it to iPhoto), Control-click the clip and choose Reveal in Finder from the contextual menu. The image is stored within the project file on disk (which normally isn't obviously accessible), but getting to it this way lets you copy the JPEG file that iMovie creates (**Figure 11.22**).

Figure 11.20 Turn any video frame into a still photo.

Figure 11.21 The freeze frame appears at the playhead so the effect appears seamless.

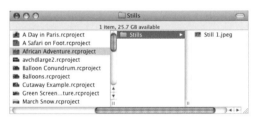

Figure 11.22 iMovie creates a new JPEG image for each still you create from video and stores it within the project file.

12

EDITING AUDIO

How important is audio in a movie? If you ever get the chance to attend an advance test screening of a Hollywood movie, the answer may be painfully clear. I've been to screenings where the audio in some scenes consisted of just what was recorded on set—no background music, no sound mixing to balance actors' voices and dampen background noise, no re-recorded dialogue to enhance enunciation. Although quite a bit of work goes into editing audio, people tend not to notice it unless something is wrong.

I covered some methods for capturing quality audio in Chapter 5, which is the first step. But audio can be much more than just video's underappreciated sibling. In this chapter, you'll see how editing audio tracks can give depth to your movie by working independently of the video, and by adding music, narration, and sound effects.

iMovie's New Audio Approach

If you're coming to iMovie '09 from iMovie HD 6, audio editing looks downright perplexing. Audio clips are no longer restricted to just two tracks below the video track, but the new interface makes that difficult to discern. Don't worry, though, it will start to make sense pretty quickly.

Unfortunately, a lot of audio functionality that finally made its way into iMovie HD 6 is absent in iMovie '09. You don't have as much control over audio within a clip, visual waveform display is gone in the main editing area, and the audio effects have also been silenced (including my favorite Noise Reducer).

Hopefully, Apple will roll these functions into later versions of iMovie or open up the program to third-party developers who can restore those functions. In the meantime, you can always export video from iMovie '09, import it into GarageBand, and edit the audio there.

Changing a Clip's Volume

When you import footage, the video and audio are combined in the filmstrip. As you're editing video clips, you're also editing the audio—splitting, trimming, and cropping it with the visuals. You can control how loud an individual clip plays using the Audio Adjustments panel of the Inspector.

If there's a lot of variation in the volume of the clips, you can also *normalize* them, which balances each clip to roughly the same level.

To increase or decrease a clip's volume:

1. Double-click the clip you want to edit in either the Project Browser or the Event Browser to bring up the Inspector, and then click the Audio button. Or, click the Inspector button on the toolbar and then select a clip to edit. My preferred option is to select a clip and just press the A key.

   The Audio Adjustments panel of the Inspector appears.

2. Drag the Volume slider to increase or decrease the clip's volume (**Figure 12.1**).

3. Press the Spacebar to play back the clip, starting at the playhead location. Keep an eye on the volume indicators in the toolbar (**Figure 12.2**). If the levels are pushing into the red zone, your audio is too loud and should be turned down.

To normalize a clip's volume:

1. Select a clip and bring up the Audio Adjustments panel of the Inspector.

2. Click the Normalize Clip Volume button. iMovie automatically adjusts the volume. The thumbnail icon identifies the type of edit applied (**Figure 12.3**).

✔ Tip

- Select multiple clips to apply the same edit to all of them at once.

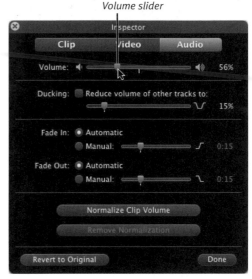

Volume slider

Figure 12.1 Adjusting the Volume slider affects the audio of an entire clip.

Figure 12.2 The volume indicators make it easy to see if your audio is too loud.

Volume adjusted   *Audio normalized*

Figure 12.3 Unique icons indicate audio adjustments.

Drag to set duration

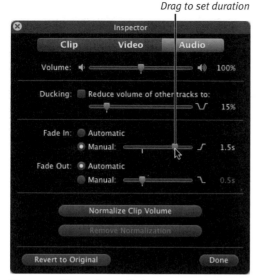

Figure 12.4 You can't specify the amount of fade—it's either silent or whatever is set in the Volume slider—but you can determine how long the fade will last, up to two seconds.

Fading Audio In or Out

One of the more common audio effects is to fade the sound in from silence at the beginning of a scene, or fade it out at the end.

To fade audio in or out:

1. Select a clip and bring up the Audio Adjustments panel of the Inspector.

2. Drag the Fade In or Fade Out slider to set the duration of the fade. For example, to start the clip silent and bring it to full volume over the course of 1.5 seconds, drag the Fade In slider to the 1.5s mark (**Figure 12.4**).

3. Click Done to exit the Inspector.

✔ Tips

- Moving the Fade In or Fade Out slider enables the Manual radio button; you don't have to click it separately.

- With the tool still selected, you can click another clip and edit its settings without closing the Audio Adjustments panel.

- When you apply a Fade In or Fade Out transition (see the next chapter), the audio automatically fades to accompany the visual effect.

- The controls in the Audio Adjustments panel also apply to audio-only clips (covered in the next several pages) as well as to video clips.

- Unfortunately, the fade controls are amazingly limited, especially if you're used to the freedom afforded by iMovie HD 6. I hope some of the features found in the old version migrate to the new.

Adding Music

I suppose I should have titled this section "Adding Audio Files," but iMovie is really geared toward adding music from iTunes or GarageBand. If you're familiar with other video editing software, one of the first things you may have noticed in iMovie '09 was the lack of distinct audio tracks beneath the video track. It turns out, however, that the tracks are just hidden from view.

iMovie treats music and audio in two ways: Background music literally appears as if it's behind the filmstrip, while other audio clips are attached to the bottom of the filmstrip.

To locate songs in your iTunes or GarageBand libraries:

1. Click the Music and Sound Effects button in the toolbar or choose Music and Sound Effects from the Window menu (or just press Command-1).

2. Click iTunes or GarageBand in the source list. Your library appears in the preview area (**Figure 12.5** and **Figure 12.6**); click the triangle beside either name to view your playlists.

3. Scroll through the list to find the song you want to use.

   Or, type a word in the Search field if you're looking for a particular song or artist name. The list updates as you type (**Figure 12.7**). Click the Cancel button (with the white X on it) to clear the field and return to the full list.

✔ Tips

- The Search field returns matches for all iTunes metadata, not just titles and artists.

- Set up a custom iMovie playlist in iTunes that contains the music you want to use for a particular project to help you find songs faster.

Figure 12.5 Narrow your song list by clicking the name of a playlist.

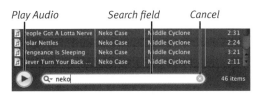

Figure 12.6 When viewing the GarageBand list, you can preview songs with a full guitar icon. The songs with document icons must be saved again in GarageBand with an iLife preview before you can play or import them in iMovie.

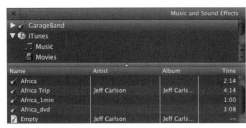

Figure 12.7 Type the name of a song or artist into the Search field to display only the matches in the list.

Figure 12.8 Five columns can be viewed at once.

Figure 12.9 You can also view the song list by icon, which uses the album art (when available).

Artist	Album	Time
Badly Drawn Boy	About A Boy	0.21
London Symp...	Star Wars: A New ...	0.22
DeVotchKa	How It Ends	0.25
David Arnold ...	Casino Royale (Or...	0.26
Robert Shaw ...	Messiah (1 of 2) ...	0.27
David Arnold ...	Casino Royale (Or...	0.27

Figure 12.10 Sorting the library by time makes it easy to find music that matches the length of your video clips or sequences.

Audio Copyright

It's worth pointing out that most songs you import from iTunes are probably copyrighted material. For most people this is no problem, since only friends and family are likely to see their edited movies. But if you're planning to distribute the movie or play it for a lot of people, you need to get permission to use the music.

To add audio files from the Finder:

◆ Drag an audio file from the Finder directly to the Project Browser.

To customize the song list:

◆ In the list view, Control-click in the song list, go to Show Columns, and choose which columns are visible (**Figure 12.8**).

◆ Click and drag a column heading to change the order in which it appears.

◆ Control-click in the song list and choose Display as Icons to view the songs by their album artwork (**Figure 12.9**).

To listen to a song:

1. Select a song in the list.

2. Click the round Play Audio button to play the track from the beginning. Click the button again to stop playing.

✔ Tips

■ Click a column heading to sort the song list (**Figure 12.10**). For example, I often click the Time column to find songs that fit within a given section of a movie.

■ You can make any folder of songs appear in the Audio list: simply drag the folder from the Finder to the top pane in the browser. It appears in a Folders folder.

■ iMovie can import any file format that iTunes can play, so you're not limited to just MP3 files.

■ Music encoded in MP3 or AAC format in iTunes is compressed, meaning that some audio data have been removed to make the file size smaller. Most people probably won't notice the difference, but some audiophiles can tell. If you need to use the highest-quality music in your movies, import the songs in AIFF format within iTunes.

Adding background music

The idea behind background music is that it enables you to quickly throw some tunes behind your video without the hassle of positioning clips on an audio track. iMovie's implementation is a clever interface, though not entirely intuitive if you want to do more with those clips.

To add background music:

1. Drag one or more songs from the song list to a space in the Project Browser that is *outside the filmstrip* (**Figure 12.11**). The background turns green to indicate that you're adding background music.

   When you play your movie, the music plays behind the audio belonging to the video clips.

   If the song file is longer than the movie, it's faded out at the end and marked with a musical note icon to indicate there's more music available (**Figure 12.12**).

2. Drag more music to the background as you see fit. iMovie slots them together so they play consecutively (**Figure 12.13**).

   The clips can be moved and edited in the background; see "Locking Background Audio" and "Trimming Audio Clips," later in this chapter.

To rearrange background music clips:

1. Choose Arrange Music Tracks from the Edit menu. Unlike most objects in iMovie, background audio cannot be rearranged by dragging (as you'll see shortly).

2. In the dialog that appears, ignore the top purple section for now and focus on the lower green section. Click a song title and drag it up or down in the list to change the order (**Figure 12.14**).

3. Click OK to make the change and find the clips repositioned in the Project Browser.

Background music indicator

Figure 12.11 When you drag a song to the area around the filmstrip, it's added as background music.

Figure 12.12 The music note icon tells you that more audio is available, but you're at the end of the video.

First song   *Next song*

Figure 12.13 A newly-added background song (selected here for emphasis) automatically falls into place after the previous one.

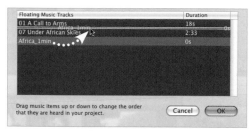

Figure 12.14 Reorder background clips in this dialog.

Figure 12.15 For non-background music clips, drag the audio file directly to the filmstrip.

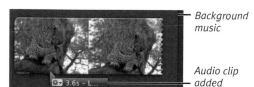

Background music

Audio clip added

Figure 12.16 Audio clips are anchored to the bottom of the video.

Figure 12.17 So much for the old two-track limitation.

Adding other audio clips

All other audio clips, such as sound effects, are anchored to the filmstrip.

To add other audio clips:

1. In the Music and Sound Effects Browser, locate the audio clip you'd like to add to the movie. (iMovie includes a set of sound effects, for example, but you're not limited to effects.)

2. Drag the sound file from the list to the place on the filmstrip where you want the audio to begin (**Figure 12.15**). The Viewer displays the frame beneath the playhead to help you position the clip more accurately.

   The audio clip appears fastened to the bottom of the filmstrip as a green bar (**Figure 12.16**).

   You can continue adding audio clips and building layers of audio tracks. Simply drag and drop new clips on the filmstrip. iMovie stacks them visually from longest (closest to the filmstrip itself) to shortest to make it obvious where they begin and end (**Figure 12.17**).

To reposition audio clips:

1. Click an audio clip to select it.

2. Drag the clip to a new position. The Viewer displays the frame under the playhead, which is also where iMovie places the anchor point.

✔ Tips

- By default, iMovie snaps the end of an audio clip to edit points such as the beginnings or endings of video and other audio clips. Choose Snap to Ends from the View menu to disable this behavior.

- See Chapter 10 for instructions on offsetting audio clips in the Precision Editor.

ADDING MUSIC

Recording Voiceovers

I read that while shooting *Crouching Tiger, Hidden Dragon*, actor Chow Yun Fat (who doesn't speak Mandarin Chinese natively) didn't put much work into pronouncing his dialogue correctly during filming. Instead, he fine-tuned his accent when re-recording the dialogue in post production. Most likely you won't be doing much re-recording (also called *looping*), but iMovie's narration capability lets you add voiceovers or other sounds directly to your movie.

To record a voiceover:

1. Connect a microphone to your Mac, if necessary.

2. Click the Voiceover button in the toolbar to bring up the Voiceover window (**Figure 12.18**).

3. If you've not already done so, choose an input source from the Record From pop-up menu.

4. Adjust the Input Volume slider to accommodate for the microphone's sensitivity; if the audio levels are low as you speak, increase the volume percentage, or pull back on the slider if the levels are too high.

5. Set the Noise Reduction slider to filter out ambient noise. You'll record less noise with the slider further to the right.

6. The Voice Enhancement checkbox processes the audio with algorithms geared toward spoken-word recording; uncheck the box if you prefer the sound unprocessed (you'll have to experiment to see which version you prefer).

Voiceover button

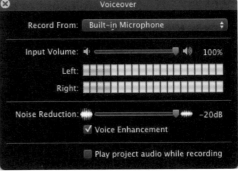

Figure 12.18 The Voiceover window displays the current microphone input levels.

Recording started *Current playhead position*

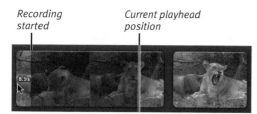

Figure 12.19 The filmstrip turns red to indicate you're currently recording a voiceover.

Voiceover recorded

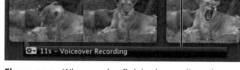

Figure 12.20 When you've finished recording, the voiceover appears as a purple audio clip.

Figure 12.21 Multiple voiceovers appear as additional audio tracks; delete the ones that didn't turn out well.

7. Enable the last item, Play project audio while recording, if you're listening to the project through headphones and need to pick up audio cues.

8. Click the point on the filmstrip where you want the recording to begin. iMovie counts down 3 seconds before that point and begins recording.

9. Speak into the microphone. The filmstrip turns red to indicate where recording has taken place (**Figure 12.19**).

10. Click within the Project Browser, or press the Esc button, to stop recording. A new audio clip, which can be edited just like other audio clips, is now attched to the filmstrip (**Figure 12.20**).

11. To record another voiceover, click another clip. Or, click the Voiceover button in the toolbar again to disable the tool.

To delete a voiceover:

◆ Click a clip to select it, and then press the Delete key or choose Delete Selection from the Edit menu.

✔ Tips

■ You can record multiple takes, then delete the ones you don't end up using (**Figure 12.21**).

■ Some Mac models do not include an audio-in port or a built-in microphone, unfortunately. Instead, consider buying an inexpensive USB audio device such as the iMic, from Griffin Technology (www.griffintechnology.com).

RECORDING VOICEOVERS

Locking Background Audio

Most audio clips are "locked" by default: they remain attached to the point on the filmstrip where you placed them. Background music clips, by contrast, start at the first frame of your movie and are pressed together like cans in a vending machine. However, you can move background audio clips and *pin* (lock) them to a specific frame of video.

To pin a background audio clip:

1. Click a background audio clip to select it (**Figure 12.22**).

2. Drag the clip to where you want it pinned to the video (**Figure 12.23**). The green floating background audio clip becomes a purple pinned clip that remains attached to that frame of video.

   Oddly, any unpinned clips that follow the pinned audio will fill in the gap left open when you dragged the mouse (**Figure 12.24**). Furthermore, that clip is trimmed to occupy only the duration of the gap.

To unpin a background audio clip:

1. Select the pinned clip.

2. Choose Unpin Music Track from the Edit menu or the contextual menu.

✔ Tips

■ If you unpin the clip in Figure 12.24, it does not return to its former position, but now appears at the end of the background music. However, clip 2 in that example regains its full duration.

■ Remember that you can use the Audio Adjustments panel to modify volume and fades of background audio tracks.

■ iMovie creates a 1-second crossfade between adjoining background audio clips.

Figure 12.22 This background music clip runs after the previous clip, but we want to pin it to the next video clip.

Figure 12.23 Dragging the clip pins it to the video, noted by a small pin icon and purple color.

Before

After

Figure 12.24 When you pin a background clip (1) that has another clip following it (2), the later clip fills in the space vacated by the pinned clip.

Ducking slider

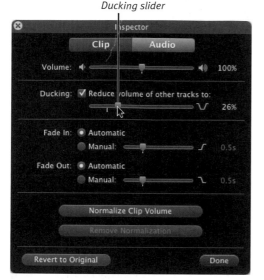

Figure 12.25 Ducking reduces the volume in other clips so you can feature the audio in the selected clip.

Ducking Audio

When you're working with multiple layers of sound, at some point there's just too much audio competing against itself. To draw attention to the audio of one clip, enable ducking, which reduces the volume of other audio for the duration of that clip. Ducking is often used to hear dialog: when someone starts talking, the background music fades (but doesn't go silent).

To duck audio:

1. Click a video or audio clip to select it. Background audio clips cannot be ducked.

2. Double-click the clip and click the Audio button (or press the A key) to bring up the Audio Adjustments panel of the Inspector.

3. Click the Ducking checkbox to enable the feature (**Figure 12.25**). The volume of surrounding clips is reduced to 15 percent of their volume setting.

4. Drag the Ducking slider to make the other clips louder (drag to the right) or softer (drag to the left).

5. Click Done to exit the window.

✔ Tip

■ iMovie automatically applies fades when ducking, so the surrounding audio smoothly drops down to the ducking level at the start of the clip and then goes back up to full volume at the end.

Trimming Audio Clips

As with video, you can trim audio clips to the duration that works best for your project. For quick adjustments, simply drag the edges in the Project Browser. For more precise edits, or to edit background music clips, open the clip in the trimmer.

Figure 12.26 The pointer's icon changes to indicate that you can trim the audio clip.

To trim an audio clip in the Project Browser:

1. Position the mouse pointer at the left or right edge of the audio clip. The pointer becomes a double-ended arrow icon (**Figure 12.26**).

Figure 12.27 Drag to change the duration of the clip.

2. Click and drag to reveal or hide the audio (**Figure 12.27**).

To trim an audio clip in the trimmer:

1. Select an audio clip and choose Clip Trimmer from the Action menu, or press Command-R.

   The Clip Trimmer appears in place of the Event Browser (**Figure 12.28**). The lighter-colored area indicates the audible portion of the clip.

Figure 12.28 The Clip Trimmer displays the audio clip with waveforms to help you make more precise edits.

2. Drag the yellow handles to set the start and end points of the clip. The waveforms will help you locate where dialog begins and ends, for example. As you drag, the Viewer displays the video frame beneath the playhead.

   If you're trimming a background audio clip that has been automatically shortened due to a pinned clip (see Figure 12.24, earlier), iMovie displays the audible portion of the waveforms in a light color and the inaudible portions in black (**Figure 12.29**). However, because the clip is being trimmed automatically by iMovie, the end point does not change.

End of audible portion

Figure 12.29 Trimming a background music clip.

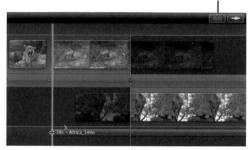

Figure 12.30 Drag the middle of the selection to slip the clip and retain the same duration.

Show or Hide Extras

Figure 12.31 You can change duration and position of audio clips in the Precision Editor.

3. To slip the clip (adjust the start and end points without changing the clip's duration), click the middle of the selection and drag (**Figure 12.30**).

4. Press the Play button to play back the clip (which also includes any other audio at the same location in the filmstrip) or click Done to exit the Clip Trimmer.

To trim an audio clip in the Precision Editor:

1. Double-click the space between two clips, or choose Precision Editor from a clip's Action menu to open the Precision Editor.

2. In the editor, click the Show or Hide Extras button (**Figure 12.31**).

3. Drag the edges of the audio clip to change its duration, or drag the clip itself to change its position. Click Done.

✔ Tip

■ You don't have to select an audio clip before you trim it. When you click and drag a clip's edge, it's automatically selected for you.

TRIMMING AUDIO CLIPS

Adding Just the Audio from a Video Clip

Sometimes you may want just the audio portion of a video clip. For example, let's say your stepbrother captured better audio of your sister's wedding on his camcorder, but your vantage point made for better visuals. You can easily insert the audio from his footage.

To add audio from a video clip:

1. Select a video clip (or portion of a clip) in the Event Browser.

2. Drag the clip to the point in the Project Browser's filmstrip at which you want the audio to appear (**Figure 12.32**).

3. From the pop-up menu that appears, choose Audio Only (**Figure 12.33**).

   The audio from the video clip appears as a new audio clip pinned to the filmstrip (**Figure 12.34**).

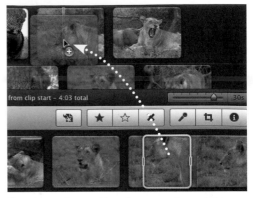

Figure 12.32 Drag a video clip on top of an existing clip, even if you want to add just the audio portion.

Figure 12.33 Hold Command-Shift while dragging a video clip to the Project Browser to add just the audio.

Figure 12.34 Instead of inserting the video at the playhead, the audio appears pinned to that spot.

TRANSITIONS AND TITLES

Transitions can be equally wonderful and terrible things. They can move you from one scene to another without the abruptness of a straightforward cut, or help define a movie's pace by easing you gently into or out of a scene.

But transitions can also become a distraction, because you're introducing motion or visuals that weren't recorded by the camera. Too many transitions can be like using too many fonts in a word processing application: pretty soon, all you see is the style, not the content.

Titles, however, are another story. In Hollywood, movie titles aren't mere words that flash up on the screen. Actors, agents, and studio executives negotiate for the length of time a person's name appears, how large or small the typeface is, whether the name comes before or after the movie title, and all sorts of other conditions that inflame my aversion to fine print. You won't deal with any of that, because the other aspects of movie titles—i.e., actually *creating* them— are made extraordinarily easy in iMovie.

As with a lot of iMovie capabilities, you're creating elements quickly and cheaply that used to cost a fortune for studios and filmmakers.

Adding Transitions

Adding a transition to your movie is as easy as dragging and dropping an icon. You can then edit the transition in place (and best of all, you don't have to wait for it to render as in the old days of iMovie).

To add a transition:

1. Click the Transitions button in the toolbar, choose Transitions from the Window menu, or press Command-4. The Transitions Browser appears to the right of the Event Browser (**Figure 13.1**).

2. Choose a transition from the browser. Each icon plays a preview of its effect when you move your pointer over it.

3. Drag the transition to the intersection of two clips in the Project Browser (**Figure 13.2**). (Transitions can be added to the beginning and end of the movie as well; the image transitions between the video clip and black.) A transition icon appears (**Figure 13.3**).

To change a transition's style:

◆ Drag a new style from the Transitions Browser onto an existing one.

◆ Hold Option and drag one transition in your project onto another.

or

1. Double-click a transition to bring up the Inspector, or press I. You can also select the transition and click the Inspector button on the toolbar.

2. Click the Transition button.

3. From the grid of available transitions that appears, click one to apply (**Figure 13.4**). This approach lets you preview the transition in the Viewer.

4. Click Done to exit the Inspector.

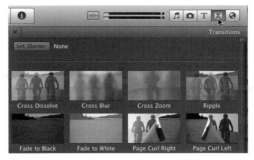

Figure 13.1 Choose from a variety of transition effects in the Transitions Browser.

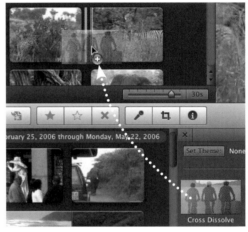

Figure 13.2 Drag a transition icon to your project.

Figure 13.3 Transitions appear in the filmstrip as small icons between clips.

ADDING TRANSITIONS

Figure 13.4 Choose a new transition from within the Inspector.

Figure 13.5 Change a transition's duration in this dialog instead of dragging endpoints in the browser.

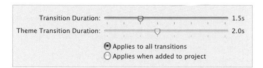

Figure 13.6 The Transition Duration slider applies to all transitions in the project or to new ones as they are added.

Theme Transitions

Themes rely heavily on transitions, using motion graphics to put scenes into a larger visual context. I discuss working with theme transitions in Chapter 14, "Themes and Maps."

To delete a transition:

1. Select the transition in the Project Browser.

2. Press the Delete key, or choose Cut or Clear from the Edit menu. The sections of clips used by the transition are restored.

To change a transition's duration:

1. Double-click a transition in the movie or press I to display the Inspector.

2. Enter a new time in the Duration field (**Figure 13.5**).

   If you want every transition in the project to share the same duration, mark the Applies to all transitions checkbox.

To change the default duration of transitions:

1. If you prefer that all new transitions be longer than the default half-second amount, choose Project Properties from the File menu or the contextual menu, or press Command-J.

2. In the Project Properties dialog, click the Timing button and set a new time in the Transition Duration slider (**Figure 13.6**).

3. Choose how the setting will be applied: to all transitions in the project or to transitions added from that point forward.

4. Click OK to apply the settings. If you chose Applies to all transitions, the durations of existing transitions are changed.

✔ Tip

■ You can move a transition to another spot in the filmstrip by dragging it to the new location. Hold Option as you drag to create a copy of the transition—it doesn't copy any of the footage, but applies its style and duration to the new clips that surround it.

To automatically add transitions:

1. Choose Project Properties from the File menu or press Command-J.

2. Mark the Automatically add checkbox (**Figure 13.7**).

3. Choose a style from the pop-up menu. (If you don't see a pop-up menu, make sure the Theme is set to None.)

4. Choose one option below the checkbox:

   ▲ **Overlap ends and shorten clip.** iMovie uses the visible footage to generate the transition, resulting in a shorter clip (see the sidebar opposite).

   ▲ **Extend ends and maintain duration (where possible).** iMovie uses excess footage that's outside the trim points to build the transition.

5. Click OK to apply the transitions throughout the project. When automatic transitions are enabled, you can't delete them manually.

To turn off automatic transitions:

1. Choose Project Properties from the File menu or press Command-J.

2. Disable the Automatically add checkbox.

3. In the dialog that appears, choose how iMovie handles the footage that the transitions were using (**Figure 13.8**).

   If you choose Leave transitions in current locations, you can selectively delete the ones you no longer want to keep.

✔ Tips

■ Leave enough padding in your clips to accommodate transitions. Otherwise, your transitions won't display correctly.

■ Each transition type has its own icon in the Project Browser, making it easy to see at a glance which style is applied.

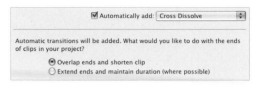

Figure 13.7 If you prefer to let iMovie do all the work, set it to add transitions automatically in the project.

Figure 13.8 Turning off automatic transitions.

Most Valuable Transitions

In most situations, you'll find yourself using only a couple of transitions: Cross Dissolve and Fade to Black. I'm also partial to Fade to White, in the right context. The others, to me, are usually too flashy for regular use.

The Fade to Black transition does double duty: Putting it at the beginning of the movie gives you a fade-in; at the end, you get a fade-out. You're essentially transitioning from nothing (black) to the first clip and vice-versa for the last clip.

iMovie's Habit of Stealing Time

As you add transitions, you may notice something odd happening: your movie is getting *shorter*. Is it possible to add things to a movie and still end up with less than when you started? (And if so, does it apply to eating ice cream?)

Yes. (But no to the ice cream.) Here's how iMovie steals time using transitions (**Figure 13.9**):

1. For the sake of not straining my math abilities, let's assume we want to add a Cross Dissolve transition between two 10-second clips. In order to maintain a comfortable pace, we decide to make our transition 2 seconds long.

2. We drag the transition into place between the clips, and notice that each clip has become 8 seconds in length, not 9 seconds (to split a 2-second transition between two clips leaves 1 second for each clip: $10 - 1 = 9$).

3. The mystery is solved when we look at how iMovie is building the transition. It needs to start dissolving one clip into the other clip at the very beginning of the transition, so iMovie merges 2 seconds of each clip, removing 4 seconds total. The transition is still 2 seconds in duration, but requires 4 seconds to perform the blends. Think of it as tightening a belt: you still have the same amount of material, but the overlap where the buckle rests allows you to encompass a smaller area.

Total movie time before transition: 20 seconds

Clips before adding transition

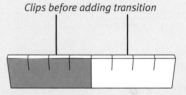

Total movie time decreases to 18 seconds after adding transition

Two-second transition steals a total of four seconds from the affected clips.

Overlap at point of transition

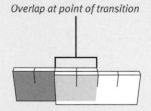

Figure 13.9 Some transitions, such as Cross Dissolve, need to overlap two clips in order to merge the number of frames needed for the effect. This creates a shorter overall movie.

To edit a transition in the Precision Editor:

1. Double-click the space above a transition or choose Precision Editor from the Action pop-up menu (**Figure 13.10**). The Precision Editor opens.

2. Choose any of the following editing actions:

   ▲ Drag the right or left edge of the transition icon to change the duration (**Figure 13.11**). The Viewer displays the frame below the playhead.

   ▲ To reposition (slip) the transition, drag the middle of its icon.

   ▲ As when editing video clips in the Precision Editor, drag the first (leftmost) cut point in the top or bottom clip to keep the position of the transition in that clip while adjusting the position of the other clip.

   ▲ With audio waveforms visible, drag the first cut point in the video's accompanying audio portion to offset the audio transition (**Figure 13.12**). Hold Shift to move the offset for both video clips.

   ▲ Double-click the transition to open the Inspector, where you can change its duration and style.

3. Click Done to exit the Precision Editor.

✔ Tips

■ If there isn't enough video in a source clip to give a transition the duration you want, the time appears in orange text. To fix, open the Precision Editor and reposition one of the clips to compensate.

■ See Chapter 10 for more information on using the Precision Editor.

Figure 13.10 A transition's Action menu appears in the space below the transition icon.

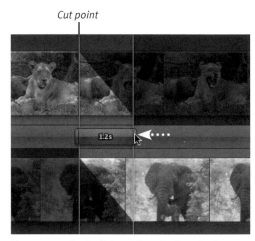

Figure 13.11 The Precision Editor displays the footage occupied by the transition (the diagonal shading).

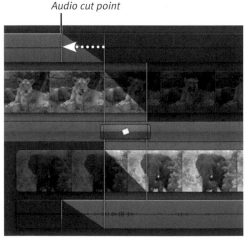

Figure 13.12 Offsetting the audio includes the audio during the transition.

ADDING TRANSITIONS

Figure 13.13 iMovie offers many title styles. Move your mouse pointer over one to preview its effect.

Title will occupy the first portion of the video clip.

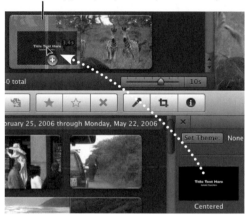

Figure 13.14 The blue highlight indicates the duration of the title when you release the mouse button.

Title clip

Figure 13.15 Titles appear as blue clips anchored above the video.

Adding Titles

In ages past, the way to add a title to a movie was to set it up in the camera laboriously, scrolling through each letter (depending on the camera model) to have the date or scene name burned to tape forever. Long before that, of course, editors shot footage of title cards that provided the "dialog" in silent movies. Thankfully, we've come a long way since then.

To add a title:

1. Click the Titles button in the toolbar, choose Titles from the Window menu, or press Command-3. The Titles Browser appears to the right of the Event Browser (**Figure 13.13**).

2. Drag a title's icon onto a clip in the Project Browser (**Figure 13.14**). The blue highlighted area indicates where the title will be applied: A partial highlight indicates the beginning or end of the clip; if the entire clip is highlighted, the title will match the duration of the clip.

   The title appears as a blue clip above the video clip (**Figure 13.15**).

3. Enter the text for the title and click Done (see "Editing Title Text" later in this chapter).

To reposition a title:

◆ Click within the title clip and drag it to a new position on the filmstrip.

✔ Tip

■ For more precise initial placement of a title, hold Shift as you drag it to the project. The blue highlight becomes four seconds in length and can be placed anywhere, not just at the start, end, or entirety of a clip.

To display a title against a custom background:

1. Drag a title to the space between two clips. The Choose Background preview palette appears (**Figure 13.16**).

2. Skim over each background style to preview it in the Viewer. Some styles, such as Underwater, are animated, while others are static images or solid colors. Click one to choose that background.

3. When you release the mouse button, a new blank clip pushes aside the clip that follows the title and displays the text on the background, rather than overlaying it on clip footage (**Figure 13.17**).

To change a title's duration:

◆ Drag the left or right edge of the title clip (**Figure 13.18**).

◆ Double-click the title to bring up the Inspector, and then enter a new time in the Duration field.

To set a title's fade duration:

1. Double-click the title to display the Inspector.

2. Drag the Fade In/Out slider to set the time it takes for the title to appear and disappear (**Figure 13.19**). The radio button automatically switches to Manual when you drag the slider. Click Done.

To set a default title fade duration:

1. Choose Project Properties from the File menu or press Command-J.

2. Click the Timing button.

3. Using the Title Fade Duration slider, choose a new value, up to 2 seconds. iMovie fades in the start of the title and fades out the end over the time you specify. Click OK.

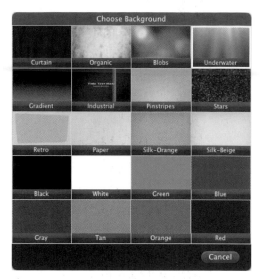

Figure 13.16 Dragging a title to the space between clips in the project gives you the option of applying it to a custom background.

New background clip

Figure 13.17 The custom background appears as a new clip in the project.

Figure 13.18 A title can span multiple clips. Simply drag the left or right edges to change its duration.

Fade In/Out slider

Figure 13.19 Control the time it takes for a title to appear and disappear.

Figure 13.20 Access the full range of titles from the Inspector, where you can preview the effects.

To change a title's style:

◆ Drag a new style from the Titles Browser onto the clip containing the existing title.

◆ Hold Option and drag one title in your project onto another clip with a title.

or

1. Double-click a title to bring up the Inspector, or press I.

2. Click the Title button.

3. From the grid that appears, click a title to apply (**Figure 13.20**).

4. Click Done to exit the Inspector.

To delete a title:

1. Select the offending title clip.

2. Press the Delete key. You can also choose Cut or Clear from the Edit menu.

✔ Tips

■ If you've added a title to an entire clip (compared to adding just to the beginning or end), changing the duration of the video clip or background also changes the length of the title.

■ Titles remain anchored to the clips they're positioned above, so if you move (or delete) the underlying clip, the title goes with it.

■ The Four Corners style offers a neat trick: add back-to-back instances of it to make each title arrive from a different corner. Unfortunately, there's no way to specify which corner each title uses.

■ Remember, not everyone may be able to read as fast as you. Give your viewers plenty of time to read your title—without boring them, of course.

■ Some title styles, such as Boogie Lights, cannot be changed.

ADDING TITLES

Editing Title Text

Unless your movie is called "Title Text Here," follow these steps to add your own text.

To edit title text:

1. Click a title in the Project Browser to select it. The Viewer becomes editable (**Figure 13.21**).

2. Click within the text to position your pointer and select the text you want to change (**Figure 13.22**).

3. Type new title text. Feel free to click the Play button to see how the text appears above the footage.

4. When you're finished editing the text (including any formatting, described just ahead), click Done.

To insert special characters:

1. Click within the text field to position the pointer.

2. Choose Special Characters from the Edit menu, or press Command-Option-T.

3. Select a character from the Characters palette.

4. Click the Insert button. The character appears in the text field (**Figure 13.23**).

✔ Tips

- When entering text for the Scrolling Credits title, you can include more than just the four placeholders provided. To get the text to line up properly, press the Tab key to insert a tab character before and after the name in the left column.

- You can't change the text (or style) of the Date/Time title, but that's okay. It displays the date and time of the clip to which it's attached, saving you the trouble of adding that information manually.

Figure 13.21 Selecting a title turns the Viewer into a text-editing environment.

Figure 13.22 The title can be edited much as if you were working in a text editor or word processor.

Figure 13.23 Take advantage of the Characters palette to locate symbols and "dingbats."

Typeface   Color   Size

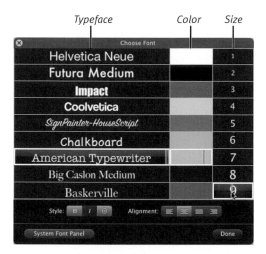

Figure 13.24 Choose a typeface, color, and size to be applied to the entire title.

Editing Text Style

Now that you've entered some text, it's time to give it style: select a color and a typeface, and change the type size. iMovie includes two methods for doing this: the iMovie Font Panel and the System Font Panel.

Using the iMovie Fonts palette

The iMovie Font Panel provides a quick and easy way to specify typeface, size, and color; and to save styles for use later.

To edit text style using the iMovie Fonts palette:

1. Click a title in the Project Browser if it's not already selected.

2. Click the Show Fonts button to bring up the Choose Font palette (**Figure 13.24**).

3. Position your mouse pointer over a typeface, color, or size to preview how the title will appear with that selection. Skimming the box lets you view the entire clip.

4. To apply a typeface, color, or size, click its box. Using the buttons at the bottom of the palette, you can also set whether the text is bold, italic, or outlined, and choose a text alignment.

5. Click Done to apply the changes.

✔ Tip

■ Note that the entire title assumes this setting. If you prefer to specify a different size for a subhead, for example, you'll need to do so in the System Font Panel.

To redefine a text style:

1. Open iMovie's preferences and click the Fonts button.

2. To replace a typeface, click the pop-up menu indicator to choose a face from those installed on your computer (**Figure 13.25**).

3. To change one of the default colors, click it to bring up the system Colors palette (**Figure 13.26**).

   Click a new color in the color wheel, then close the palette by clicking the close button in the upper-left corner.

4. Close the iMovie Preferences window to apply the changes.

   Now, you can quickly access those font settings using the iMovie Font Panel for future titles you create.

✔ Tips

■ The Colors palette also lets you change the opacity of a color, so you can specify a translucent preset color in the Fonts preferences by adjusting the Opacity slider (**Figure 13.27**).

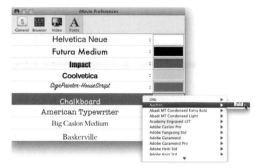

Figure 13.25 Choose a new typeface to replace one of the default styles in iMovie's preferences.

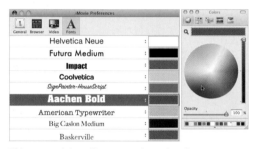

Figure 13.26 Specify a new color using the system Colors palette.

Figure 13.27 The text is translucent after changing the opacity of a preset color in iMovie's preferences.

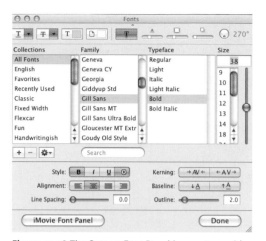

Figure 13.28 The System Font Panel is a system-wide control for formatting text.

Text Color button

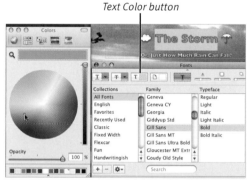

Figure 13.29 Select a text color from the Colors palette.

Figure 13.30 The typographic possibilities are extensive using the System Font Panel.

Using the system Fonts palette

The System Font Panel gives you more control over the appearance of your text.

To edit text style:

1. Click a title in the Project Browser if it's not already selected.

2. Select the text to edit.

3. Click the Show Fonts button to bring up the iMovie Fonts palette (if it's not already visible).

4. Click the System Font Panel button to switch to it (**Figure 13.28**).

To change text color:

1. In the System Font Panel, click the Text Color button. The Colors palette appears (**Figure 13.29**).

2. Click within the color wheel to select a color, or click one of the buttons at the top to change selectors (such as sliders or even Crayon colors). You can try as many colors as you like while the palette is visible, and see them applied to text in the Viewer.

3. Click the close button in the upper-left corner of the Colors palette to accept the last color you applied.

To specify font and size:

1. In the System Font Panel, choose a font and style from the Family and Typeface columns (**Figure 13.22**).

2. Drag the Size slider to increase or decrease the type size.

3. Click Done or the Hide Fonts button in the Viewer to apply the changes.

14

THEMES AND MAPS

I'm convinced that iMovie's developers at Apple talked management into letting them explore the world in the name of "research." How else to explain the several travel-focused features? (Maybe it's because so many people document their vacations on video?)

Exhibit A: themes. iMovie's themes add animated elements that frame the movie with more than just your footage—your video can become a virtual book of your experiences, to name one theme. When you apply a theme to a project, iMovie adds an opening title, an end title (complete with a "directed by" credit with your name inserted), and several theme transitions that follow the same visual idea.

Or take the more obvious Exhibit B: maps. With a small amount of work on your part, you can include a globe or flat world map that pinpoints a location and draws an animated line to the next destination.

Sounds like a pretty good gig to me. Now, where's my suitcase?

Applying a Theme

iMovie gives you the option to apply a theme when you create a project, but you can also set or change a theme at any point while editing.

To apply a theme when creating a new project:

1. Choose New Project from the File menu, or click the New Project button in the Project Library.

2. Give your project a name, specify an aspect ratio, and then click the theme you wish to apply (**Figure 14.1**).

3. When you choose a theme, the option to automatically add theme elements is enabled. If you'd rather add them manually, uncheck the Automatically add transitions and titles option.

4. Click the Create button.

To apply a theme to an existing project:

1. Open the Project Properties dialog by choose Project Properties from the File menu or pressing Command-J.

2. Click a theme to choose it.

3. If Automatically add transitions and titles is active, specify how iMovie should insert transitions: by using footage currently visible in the project, or by using footage hidden outside the edit points.

4. Click OK. iMovie adds theme titles to the start and end of your project, plus theme transitions in some places and Cross Dissolve transitions between the rest of the clips in the project (**Figure 14.3**).

   Any existing titles remain unchanged, except those at the beginning and end of the movie, which are converted to theme titles. Any existing titles are removed.

Theme selected

Figure 14.1 Choose a theme when you create a project.

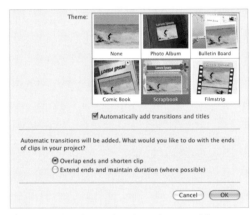

Figure 14.2 iMovie needs to know how to add new transitions when applying a theme to a project in progress.

Theme title   *Theme transition*   *Cross Dissolve*

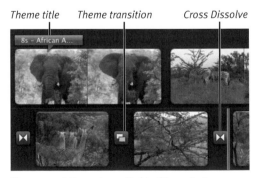

Figure 14.3 A theme is applied to this project.

Set Theme button

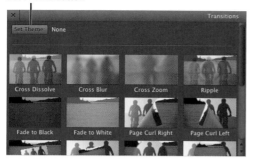

Figure 14.4 Choose a theme from the Transitions or Titles Browsers.

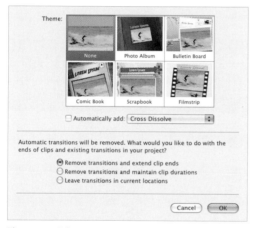

Figure 14.5 When you remove a theme from a project, choose how transitions are to be handled.

To apply a theme from the Titles or Transitions Browsers:

1. Open the Titles Browser (Command-3) or the Transitions Browser (Command-4).

2. Click the Set Theme button (**Figure 14.4**).

3. In the dialog that appears, click a Theme to choose it, and specify whether automatic transitions should be added.

4. Click OK to apply the theme.

To change a project's theme:

1. Bring up the Project Properties dialog, or click the Set Theme button in the Titles Browser or Transitions Browser.

2. Click a different theme to select it.

3. Click OK to apply the theme.

   All of the theme elements automatically change to reflect the current theme.

To remove a theme from a project:

1. Bring up the Project Properties dialog, or click the Set Theme button in the Titles Browser or Transitions Browser.

2. In the dialog that appears, click the None button (**Figure 14.5**).

3. Choose what happens to transitions:
   - ▲ **Remove transitions and extend clip ends** keeps the project's duration.
   - ▲ **Remove transitions and maintain clip durations** leaves the currently-visible portions of clips as they are, reducing the project's duration.
   - ▲ **Leave transitions in current locations** deletes any theme transitions but keeps other transitions.
   - ▲ If you want to apply transitions to every edit, enable the Automatically add checkbox.

4. Click OK to remove the theme.

APPLYING A THEME

Adding Theme Elements

iMovie can add titles and transitions automatically when you apply a theme, but you're also free to add those theme items yourself. When a project has a theme, additional titles and transitions appear in the corresponding browsers.

To add a theme title:

1. Open the Titles Browser by clicking the Titles button in the toolbar or pressing Command-3.

2. Choose a theme title, which appears above the regular titles, and drag it to a clip in your project (**Figure 14.6**).

3. Edit the title text in the Viewer (**Figure 14.7**) and then click Done.

To add a theme transition:

1. Open the Transitions Browser by clicking the Transitions button in the toolbar or pressing Command-4.

2. Choose a theme transition and drag it to a clip in your project.

To change a theme element:

◆ As with regular titles and transitions, drag a replacement element over the top of an existing one to change it.

✔ Tips

■ The theme titles don't leave much room or flexibility for long text. iMovie will reduce the text size to accommodate as best it can, but at the cost of readability.

■ For the Credits title styles, iMovie automatically fills in the name you've specified in Address Book as "My Card."

■ You can change the duration of theme titles, but not much else. Themes stick with their own built-in fonts.

Figure 14.6 Drag a theme title to your project.

Figure 14.7 Edit the text of your title.

Figure 14.8 Numbered pins in the Project Browser indicate where still frames appear in the transition.

Still frame

Figure 14.9 Moving a pin changes the frame that appears in the transition's still image.

Figure 14.10 Click to cut the pin's custom placement and return it to .its original location.

Editing Theme Transitions

The transitions in each theme follow a similar pattern: start with the previous clip filling the frame, zoom out to a collection of other images (on a bulletin board, in a scrapbook, and so forth), and then zoom in on the next clip. For transitions that display more than just two clips, iMovie chooses frames of your movie to act as still photos. Here's how to customize which images appear.

To edit a theme transition:

1. In the Project Browser, click a theme transition to select it. The Viewer displays a pulled-back view with numbered frames for the still images (**Figure 14.8**).

2. Drag a pin in the Project Browser to the frame that you want to appear as the corresponding still image (**Figure 14.9**). Repeat for as many pins as you want.

3. Click Done to exit the transition editor.

To return a pin to its original location:

1. Position the mouse pointer over a pin that has been moved; the pointer icon becomes a pair of scissors (**Figure 14.10**).

2. Click to remove the pin from the custom location.

To set a default transition duration:

1. Open the Project Properties dialog and click the Timing button.

2. Drag the Theme Transition Duration slider to set a default duration, and then click OK.

✔ Tip

■ Did the transition zip by too quickly? Extend a transition's duration to give your viewers a better look at the theme.

Creating a Map

One of the first personal videos I edited was a travelogue of a trip to Alaska. And, being a good movie geek, I wanted to replicate the effect in *Raiders of the Lost Ark* where a line pushes across a map to indicate Indy's globe-hopping. Some fiddling in Photoshop and too many hours later, I had a poor substitute.

Well, now you can get the same effect in seconds with iMovie's map features. Chart your progress across a globe or a flat map, and let iMovie figure out the details.

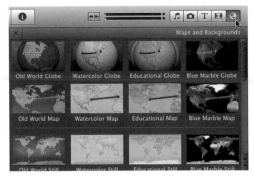

Figure 14.11 Choose from eight interactive maps. (The images below the gray line are stills and offer no interactivity.)

To create a map:

1. Click the Maps and Backgrounds button on the toolbar, choose the same item from the Window menu, or press Command-5. The Maps and Backgrounds Browser appears (**Figure 14.11**).

2. Drag a globe or map icon to your project. The map is added and the Inspector appears with a default Start Location of San Francisco (**Figure 14.12**).

3. Click the Start Location button to choose a new starting point (unless you are, in fact, starting from San Francisco). The Inspector flips over to reveal the Choose Location dialog.

4. Type a city, place name, or airport code into the search field. The list narrows as you type (**Figure 14.13**).

   If your location doesn't appear, you can enter decimal coordinates directly. (What? You don't have those handy? Go to Get Lat Lon (www.getlatlon.com) to search for a location and retrieve the coordinates.)

5. If you want the location to appear as something else (such as "Home" or "Logan's House"), type that into the Name to display on map field.

Figure 14.12 Set your map's locations in the Inspector.

Figure 14.13 iMovie recognizes 4,000 locations, which are easily found by typing in the search field.

Figure 14.14 In case you were wondering, iMovie offers you the route distance between locations.

Swap button

Figure 14.15 Click the Swap button to reverse the locations.

6. Click OK to set the location. The starting point appears with a red dot on the map.

If you just want to spotlight a single location, you can stop here. iMovie uses a subtle animation to call attention to the location.

7. To set a destination, click the Choose End Location button (which automatically enables the End Location checkbox). Choose a location using the steps outlined in Steps 4 through 6.

iMovie draws a line between the two locations and even calculates the route distance for you (**Figure 14.14**).

Press the space bar to preview the map.

8. Click Done to exit the Inspector.

✔ Tips

■ The next map you create in a project assumes the previous map's destination as the Start Location. So if your trip involved hops between multiple destinations, half the location work is done for you when you add a new map.

■ If you're mapping the return trip home, duplicate your map (choose Copy and then Paste from the Edit menu, or Option-drag the map elsewhere in your project) and then click the Swap button in the Inspector (**Figure 14.15**) to reverse the locations.

■ Unfortunately, you can't zoom in on the globe maps, so setting a trip from San Francisco to Berkeley, California, for example, makes for a boring map. The flat maps do a better job, since they can zoom in, but you won't get anywhere near the level of detail you'd find on a Google map. (That would be a great feature, though.)

■ The maps are made from high-resolution images, so they may take a few seconds to load initially.

CREATING A MAP

Editing a Map

Maps are pretty self-contained objects in iMovie—you can't apply cutaways, picture in picture, or green screen effects, for example. But there are a few things you can do with maps you've already created.

To edit a map:

1. Double-click a map, or choose Clip Adjustments from its Action menu to bring up the Inspector.

2. Click the buttons for the Start Location and End Location to change the map's destinations. You can set a new duration, apply a video effect, or swap destinations here, too.

To apply a video effect:

1. Double-click a map to open the Inspector.

2. Click the Video Effect button.

3. Click an effect from the Choose Video Effect palette to apply it (**Figure 14.16**).

4. Click Done to close the Inspector.

To change the map style:

◆ Drag a new map style from the Maps and Backgrounds Browser onto an existing map. Your duration, locations, and other settings are retained.

✔ Tips

■ You can edit a map in the Precision Editor, but doing so only changes the clip's duration; it won't let you view only a portion of the trip.

■ When you add a transition on either side of a map, the animated trip completes before the transition goes into effect.

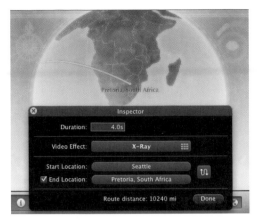

Figure 14.16 Apply a video effect to a map to give it a different appearance.

EDITING A MAP

Part 3
Sharing from iMovie

Scoring Your Movie in GarageBand

A movie's soundtrack doesn't need to consist of popular music—in fact, most films are scored instrumentally, according to the needs of each scene. If you have musical leanings, you may want to do your own scoring. With the inclusion of GarageBand in Apple's iLife suite, you can—even if you're not particularly musical, like me.

With a musical instrument and some hardware to get the audio into your Mac, you can perform your own music. Personally, I like GarageBand because I can choose from hundreds of existing background loops and create segments that are just as long as I need them to be. Those loops are also copyright- and royalty-free, so I don't need to worry about securing rights if I decide to release the movie in public.

Sharing to GarageBand

Send your entire movie to GarageBand, where you can build music with the video as reference. This option is great for timing music cues with your movie.

To share your movie to GarageBand:

1. Choose Media Browser from the Share menu.

2. Click the checkbox for the size that matches the final output of your movie (**Figure 15.1**).

3. Click the Publish button. iMovie compresses the movie and prepares it for use by the other iLife applications.

4. Launch GarageBand.

5. Choose New from the File menu; in the New Project dialog, select the Movie icon and then click Choose.

6. Give your project a name and click Create.

7. Choose Show Media Browser from the Control menu. The browser appears at the right edge of the window.

8. If it's not already visible, click the Movies button and expand the iMovie item to view the projects in the list (**Figure 15.2**). (If you didn't share the movie in Step 1, GarageBand won't display a preview.)

9. Drag the shared movie to the Timeline to add it to the project. It appears on a new video track (**Figure 15.3**).

10. Click the preview of the movie in the header of the Movie track to display the Movie Preview window.

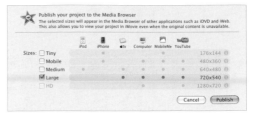

Figure 15.1 Share your movie to GarageBand to start the scoring process.

Figure 15.2 The movie you shared in iMovie is available in GarageBand's Media Browser.

Movie Track   Movie thumbnails   Movie Preview

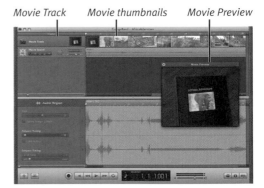

Figure 15.3 GarageBand includes your shared movie as reference to help determine timing of the music.

Mute Track button

Figure 15.4 Make the Video Sound track silent so you can focus on building the score in other tracks.

✔ Tips

- If you plan to bring the score back into iMovie for further editing (described later in this chapter), share the movie using the Mobile version; the audio settings are the same as Medium and Large, but you don't have the overhead in time and disk space required by the larger versions.

- All audio from your movie appears on one track in GarageBand, even if you had multiple tracks set up in iMovie. You may want to mute the Movie Sound track while working on your score (**Figure 15.4**).

- Having your video appear within Garage-Band is an enormous help, but it comes at a cost: even on fast machines, playback can be stuttery. GarageBand is simply a resource hog. You can regain some performance by locking audio tracks (click the padlock icon below the track name); this tells GarageBand to create a temporary "mixdown" of the locked tracks, which requires less processing power.

- I'm just scratching the surface of Garage-Band in these few pages. Be sure to read the program's online help, or pick up a good book (such as Jeff Tolbert's *Take Control of GarageBand* titles, www.takecontrolbooks.com).

Making Music Using GarageBand

With a MIDI keyboard or guitar and amp, you can start recording your own tunes. For simplicity's sake, however, I'm going to concentrate on using GarageBand's built-in loops to create a song.

To create a music loop in GarageBand:

1. Display the Loop Browser by clicking the Loop Browser button, choosing Show Loop Browser from the Control menu, or pressing Command-L (**Figure 15.5**).

2. From the first two columns of the Loop Browser, click an instrument name. You can also choose multiple musical styles (from the next two columns) to refine the list of loops. The list of available loops matching your selections appears in the pane below the browser.

3. Click a loop to hear it. The loop will continue to play until you click it again or click another loop.

4. Choose a loop and drag it to Garage-Band's Timeline to add it to your song (**Figure 15.6**).

5. Press the Play button or the spacebar to preview your song. I recommend also clicking the Cycle button (which has a picture of circled arrows) so that the song repeats as you're working. You can always hit spacebar again to stop playback.

6. The Time display shows measures, beats, and ticks. Click the small LCD mode icon in the left corner of the display to switch to Time (hours, minutes, seconds, fractions) (**Figure 15.7**).

Loop Browser   Loop Browser button

Figure 15.5 As you make instrument selections, the loop list displays loops that match your criteria.

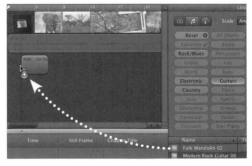

Figure 15.6 Drag a loop from the Loop Browser to GarageBand's Timeline to create a new track.

LCD mode button

Figure 15.7 I'm much more familiar with absolute time than with measures, beats, and ticks. Changing the Time display helps to define the song's length.

Region (selected)   Loop pointer

Figure 15.8 The region is the track's audio clip. Drag the edge of the region with the loop pointer to extend the duration of the loop.

Rounded corners indicate a loop within a region.

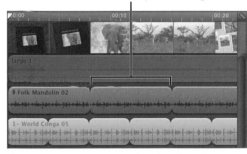

Figure 15.9 Loops are created so that they play cleanly from start to finish without breaks.

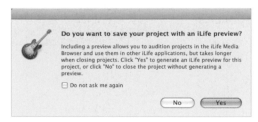

Figure 15.10 If you don't save your GarageBand project with an iLife preview, you won't be able to import the song into iMovie later.

7. Position your mouse pointer at the right edge of the loop you added, which GarageBand calls a *region*, so that the pointer changes to a rounded circle, called the *loop pointer* (**Figure 15.8**).

8. Drag the loop pointer to the right to extend the region for as long as you want it to continue playing within your song. Rounded-corner breaks within the region indicate where the loop starts and ends (**Figure 15.9**).

9. Repeat steps 2 through 4 to select another loop and add it to the Timeline as a new track. Add as many combinations as you like (guitar, drums, etc.) until the song sounds good to you.

✔ Tips

- You don't need to create a brand new track for each loop you add—they can coexist in the same tracks. But separating the tracks makes it easier to edit.

- When you close the project, GarageBand asks if you want to save an iLife preview (**Figure 15.10**). If you click Yes, iMovie will be able to import the song from the Media pane.

MAKING MUSIC USING GARAGEBAND

Getting the Score Back into iMovie

When you share your movie to GarageBand, iMovie assumes you've finished editing and are ready to hand it off. But what if you want to go back and do more editing? There's no round-trip method to automatically pass the soundtrack back to iMovie. However, it is possible to import the song manually.

To import your song into iMovie:

1. In GarageBand, mute the Movie Sound track (because it's already present in your iMovie project) and close the project.

2. In iMovie, bring up the Music and Sound Effects Browser.

3. From the audio list, choose GarageBand to display a list of your GarageBand files.

4. Drag the song you created to the Project Browser to add the song as a background music clip (**Figure 15.11**). Only songs saved with an iLife preview (indicated by a guitar icon) can be added in this way.

    You can also add GarageBand songs to the filmstrip as regular audio files, not just background music clips.

5. iMovie warns you that the published project has been modified (**Figure 15.12**); click OK.

✔ Tips

- If you change the song in GarageBand, it won't automatically be updated in iMovie. You'll need to import the Garage-Band file again.

- You may need to quit and restart iMovie for it to recognize new GarageBand songs you've created.

Figure 15.11 When you import a GarageBand song, even if it includes video footage in GarageBand, iMovie brings in only the audio.

Figure 15.12 iMovie keeps track of which version of your movie was shared; if you change it, iMovie alerts you to avoid accidental editing.

GETTING THE SCORE BACK INTO iMOVIE

SHARING TO iTUNES AND ONLINE 16

You may be creating movies that will live only on your hard disk, for your eyes only, never to be seen by anyone. More likely, though, your movies are meant to be viewed. You can export the movie to a DVD and mail it to your relatives—if you don't mind purchasing the media, filling it with movies (or just using a few minutes of it for one movie), then paying to mail it across the country or around the world. Where's the instant gratification in that?

Instead (or in addition), share your movie with the grandparents by posting it to the Web directly.

Yet another option is to transfer the movie to an iPod or iPhone. You can now show off your entire film library to your friends over lunch or coffee.

Sharing to iTunes

If you own an iPod, iPhone, or an Apple TV, the only way to get media onto it is through iTunes. iMovie can format your movies properly for those devices and ensure that you'll be able to watch your movies almost anywhere.

To share a project to iTunes:

1. Choose iTunes from the Share menu.

2. Mark one or more checkboxes for each size of movie you want to generate (**Figure 16.1**).

3. Click the Publish button. iMovie encodes the movie for the sizes you specified (**Figure 16.2**). When finished, it adds the movie to iTunes (**Figure 16.3**).

   You can then watch the movie in iTunes or synchronize your device and watch it there.

   iMovie displays an icon in the Project Library that indicates which sizes have been published, as well as a small banner in the Project Browser with the destination (**Figure 16.4**). Click the banner to switch to iTunes and view the movie there.

To remove a project from iTunes:

◆ With the project selected in the Project List, choose Remove from iTunes from the Share menu. The movie no longer appears in iTunes.

✔ Tips

■ In the Publish dialog, position the mouse pointer over the "i" icon to the right of each size to view a summary of that size's compression settings and an estimate of how much space the resulting file will be on disk.

Figure 16.1 iMovie indicates which sizes will work on which Apple (surprise!) devices.

Figure 16.2 Take a break while iMovie encodes the movie into the formats you chose.

Figure 16.3 The encoded movie appears in the Movies list.

Sizes published   *Shared destination*

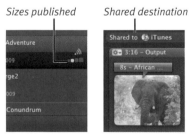

Figure 16.4 You can tell at a glance where the movie has been published.

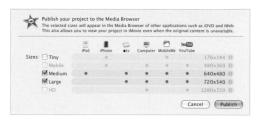

Figure 16.5 More devices are represented when you share with the Media Browser. (In this example, the Mobile option is disabled because that size was already shared.)

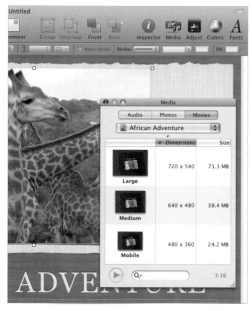

Figure 16.6 After sharing with the Media Browser, the movie appears in Keynote's Media palette.

Sharing with the Media Browser

We touched on this briefly in the last chapter, but another way to share your movie is to make it available to the Media Browser, a resource used by the iLife applications, as well as the iWork suite. The benefit of the Media Browser is that you don't have to export a file and keep track of it; supported applications know where to look.

To share with the Media Browser:

1. Choose Media Browser from the Share menu.

2. Mark one or more checkboxes for each size of movie you want to generate (**Figure 16.5**).

3. Click the Publish button. iMovie encodes the movie for the sizes you specified. When finished, the movie is available to other applications (**Figure 16.6**).

✔ Tips

- The HD size maxes out at 1280 by 720 pixels, even if you're working on 1080i or 1080p video.

- Your sharp eyes may have noticed that there's no HD option when sharing to iTunes. Although iTunes can play HD-sized content, the devices to which it currently syncs—iPods, iPhones, and the Apple TV—can't play it. (The Apple TV can handle 720p video only at 24 fps, not the NTSC standard of 30 fps or the PAL standard of 25 fps.)

- You can also share movies from the Project Library. Simply select the project you want to share—no need to open it in the Project Browser if you're not editing.

Publishing to YouTube

YouTube has emerged as a popular free destination for uploading video files and sharing them easily. iMovie lets you upload directly to YouTube, bypassing a number of hoops you'd otherwise have to jump through.

To share a movie to YouTube:

1. Choose YouTube from the Share menu.

2. In the dialog that appears, click the Add button to sign into your account. (If you don't yet have an account, you're given the opportunity to sign up.)

3. You're taken to a Web page that asks you to give iMovie permission to write content to your site. Click the Allow button, then return to iMovie and confirm the sign-in.

4. Choose a category; enter a title; and optionally write up a description of your movie. To make your movie easy for others to find, enter keywords into the Tags field (**Figure 16.7**).

5. Choose a size to publish—Mobile, Medium, Large, or HD.

6. To restrict who can view the movie, click the option marked Make this movie personal.

7. Click Next to review the YouTube Terms of Service, and then click the Publish button. After encoding and uploading the video, iMovie points you to its location on the Web (**Figure 16.8**).

   In iMovie, a banner above the movie notes that the movie has been published to YouTube, with options to tell a friend or visit the page (**Figure 16.9**).

Figure 16.7 Enter all the information about a movie here and you won't have to do it on the Web later.

Figure 16.8 Once published, your video is available to the world.

Visit button

Figure 16.9 If you forget the location of your movie, go back to iMovie and click the Visit button in the YouTube banner.

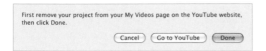

Figure 16.10 Removing a video from YouTube requires that you first manually delete the movie from YouTube.

Figure 16.11 Click Delete to purge the movie from YouTube's servers.

To remove a movie from YouTube:

1. Choose Remove from YouTube from the Share menu.

2. In the dialog that appears, click the Go to YouTube button (**Figure 16.10**).

3. On your My Videos page, locate the movie and click the Delete button (**Figure 16.11**).

4. Go back to iMovie and click the Done button. The YouTube banner is removed.

PUBLISHING TO YOUTUBE

Publishing to a MobileMe Gallery

If you subscribe to Apple's MobileMe (formerly .Mac) service, you can take advantage of its online Gallery that gives you a presence on the Web with a minimum of fuss.

To publish to a MobileMe Gallery:

1. Choose MobileMe Gallery from the Share menu.

2. In the dialog that appears, enter a title and description (**Figure 16.12**).

3. Select the sizes you want to upload. You can select as many as you'd like; your site's visitors can choose which size they want to view based on their Internet service.

4. To let people save the movie file to their hard disks, enable the option to Allow movies to be downloaded.

5. Choose an option from the Viewable by pop-up menu to determine whether the movie is private or public.

   This option also lets you set up logins and passwords so you can let only certain people view your movie.

6. Click the Hide movie on my Gallery home page checkbox to make the movie unavailable to someone who visits the main page of your Web Gallery.

7. Click Publish. iMovie encodes and uploads the movie(s). When it's finished, you can send an email announcement or visit the site directly (**Figure 16.13**). iMovie also adds a new banner to the project (**Figure 16.14**).

To remove a movie from the Gallery:

1. Choose Remove from MobileMe Gallery from the Share menu.

2. In the dialog that appears, click OK.

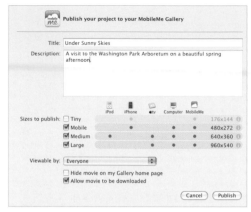

Figure 16.12 Set the options here for publishing a movie to your MobileMe Gallery.

Figure 16.13 Visitors can view and download your movies from your MobileMe Gallery.

Figure 16.14 iMovie notes where a project has been published above the filmstrip.

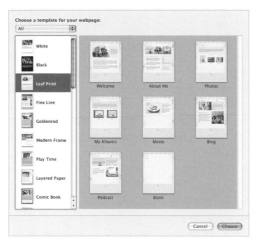

Figure 16.15 iWeb offers many ready-made Web templates, including pages designed for movies.

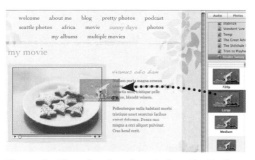

Figure 16.16 Drag the shared movie from the Media panel to the placeholder iWeb created.

Figure 16.17 Replace the sample text with your own clever musings and witty anecdotes.

Publishing to the Web Using iWeb

For more control over how the movie is presented on the Web, you can use iWeb to publish it to your Web site. iWeb uses the Media Browser to grab content from other iLife applications.

To publish to the Web using iWeb:

1. Share your movie to the Media Browser as described earlier in this chapter.

2. Launch iWeb and choose New Page from the File menu.

3. Choose a theme from the column at the left (**Figure 16.15**).

4. Click the Choose button. iWeb creates a new page.

5. Click the Show Media button to bring up the Media panel if it's not already visible.

6. Click the Movies button in the Media panel and locate your movie.

7. Drag the icon for the movie to the place-holder on the iWeb page (**Figure 16.16**).

8. Type the page title, movie title, and page description text in the fields provided (**Figure 16.17**).

9. Click the Publish Site button to create and upload the new page to your site.

To make changes to your page:

1. In iWeb, load the page by clicking its page icon in the left column.

2. Make any changes you want on the page. The page icon turns red to indicate that it's been edited but not published.

3. Click the Publish Site button.

Writing HTML

iWeb makes it extremely easy to publish movies to the Web, but you may already have a site set up, you aren't a .Mac member, or you just like to dig into the code out of pure textual geeky joy.

This, of course, isn't a book about HTML, so I'm going to assume that you know the basics about coding Web pages, and that you have an application (such as Bare Bones Software's BBEdit, or even TextEdit) that you use to build pages. If that's not the case, check out Elizabeth Castro's book *HTML for the World Wide Web with XHTML and CSS: Visual QuickStart Guide*, which remains the best HTML guide I've read.

That said, there are two ways of going about it: You can copy the file to your Web directory (provided by your Internet service provider) then link directly to it; or you can embed the movie on a Web page so that it's part of the page's layout.

To link to a QuickTime movie file:

1. In your HTML editing application, enter the following code where you want your movie link to appear. The user will see only the linked text; clicking it will download the movie.

   ```
   <a href="http://www.youraddress.com/sample.mov">Click here</a>
   ```

2. Insert the real names of your Web address and movie filename in place of *youraddress.com* and *sample.mov* (**Figure 16.18**). For example, a movie on my Web site would look like this (go ahead and put the URL below into your Web browser to view the movie):

   ```
   <a href="http://www.necoffee.com/imovievqs/secretmovie.mov">Is it really a secret?</a>
   ```

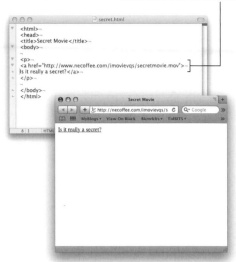

HTML text that creates link

Figure 16.18 Add a simple Web link that points to your QuickTime movie file. The HTML text in the top window creates the Web page in the bottom window.

Deciphering HTML Attributes

So what is all that junk I threw in there? Here's a breakdown of the tag attributes:

OBJECT CLASSID: To work properly under Windows, a QuickTime movie must be defined as an object. The CLASSID value identifies the content as a Quick-Time movie.

WIDTH and **HEIGHT**: These values tell the browser the width and height of your movie in pixels.

CODEBASE: This URL gives Internet Explorer for Windows some necessary information about the QuickTime format.

PARAM: This is a parameter of the object, which consists of a name and a value. SRC is the URL that points to your movie file; AUTOPLAY tells the browser whether to automatically play the movie when it loads (in this case "true" means yes); CONTROLLER tells the browser whether to display the QuickTime controller beneath the movie (in this case "false" means no).

EMBED: This is the tag that actually puts your QuickTime movie on the page. It includes the same attributes as PARAM, though in a slightly more compact fashion. A Web page that contains only this tag will display the movie correctly in all Web browsers except Internet Explorer 5.5 and later for Windows.

PLUGINSPAGE: This tells the browser where to go in the event that the QuickTime plug-in is not installed.

</EMBED> and **</OBJECT>**: These are closing tags, indicating the end of the commands.

To embed the movie on a page:

◆ In your HTML editing application, enter the following code where you want the movie to appear. Be sure to change the two instances of sample.mov to your actual filename, plus the two instances where the width and height are defined.

```
<OBJECT CLASSID="clsid:02BF25D5-8C17-
4B23-BC80-D3488ABDDC6B" WIDTH="160"
HEIGHT="144"
CODEBASE="http://www.apple.com/
qtactivex/qtplugin.cab">
<PARAM name="SRC" VALUE="sample.mov">
<PARAM name="AUTOPLAY" VALUE="true">
<PARAM name="CONTROLLER"
VALUE="false">
<EMBED SRC="sample.mov" WIDTH="160"
HEIGHT="144" AUTOPLAY="true"
CONTROLLER="false" PLUGINSPAGE=
"http://www.apple.com/quicktime/
download/">
</EMBED>
</OBJECT>
```

Note that the unintelligible gobbledygook following CLASSID= must be entered exactly as shown; it's required for viewing the page properly in Microsoft Internet Explorer 5.5 and later under Windows.

WRITING HTML

Creating a Poster Movie

Accessing a QuickTime movie on the Web introduces one big problem. Whether you link to it directly or embed it onto a page, the entire movie begins downloading. Depending on the size of the movie, this could slow your browser or other Internet applications while the movie is being fetched.

As an alternative, create a poster movie, which displays a one-frame movie that your visitors can click to initiate the download. (Sometimes this can be frustrating. I've clicked on links expecting the movie to load in the background while I'm working on something else, only to realize that I needed to then click the poster movie to get the download started. At least this route gives the visitor the option to start the movie at her convenience.) The poster movie has the added benefit of preloading the QuickTime plug-in before the movie starts.

Creating a poster movie involves two steps: creating the one-frame movie using Quick-Time Player (the Pro version), then adjusting the EMBED tag in the HTML to handle it properly.

To create the poster movie:

1. Open your movie in QuickTime Player.

2. Use the movie control buttons or the location indicator to find a frame you'd like to use as the poster movie's image (**Figure 16.19**).

3. Choose Copy from the Edit menu, or press Command-C. This copies the selected frame.

4. Create a new movie by choosing New (Command-N) from the File menu.

5. Choose Paste (Command-V) from the Edit menu. Your copied frame appears as its own one-frame movie.

Figure 16.19 Use the Playhead in QuickTime Player to locate the frame you'd like to use for the poster movie.

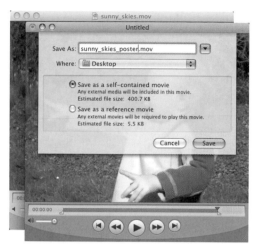

Figure 16.20 To make the poster movie work, your one frame needs to be saved as a QuickTime movie, not as an individual image format like TIFF or JPEG.

Figure 16.21 The end result is a single image that shows up in place of the movie, but one you can click to immediately begin playing the movie.

6. Save the movie with a distinctive name, such as "sunny_skies_poster.mov", to use my example (**Figure 16.20**).

To embed the poster movie:

1. In your HTML editor, type the code you used to embed the movie (shown two pages back).

2. In the EMBED tag, add the HREF and TARGET attributes (highlighted):

```
<EMBED SRC="sample_poster.
mov" WIDTH="160" HEIGHT="144"
AUTOPLAY="true"
CONTROLLER="false" HREF="sample.mov"
TARGET="myself" PLUGINSPAGE=
"http://www.apple.com/quicktime/
download/">
```

The EMBED tag tells the browser to first load the poster movie; the HREF tag tells it to load the real movie when clicked; and the TARGET tag instructs it to play the real movie in the same space as the poster movie.

3. Save and upload your files. When you view them in a Web browser, the poster image shows up first (**Figure 16.21**).

✔ Tips

■ If you're seeing only half of the movie controller, add 15 to the height values in the OBJECT and EMBED tags.

■ Be sure the controller attributes are set to "false," or else you'll see a controller in the poster movie, which can be confusing. Viewers might click the controller to play the movie, which works—but only plays the one frame.

■ It's a good idea to include instructions near the poster movie that say something like, "Click to play movie."

EXPORTING MOVIES

Publishing your movies online isn't the only method of sharing them. iMovie can export them to various formats on your hard disk for use in other applications, or to give you more control over the movies' quality. It does this through Apple's QuickTime technology.

On the surface, QuickTime is a great little utility for playing movies on your Mac. I often visit www.apple.com/trailers/ to see which new movie trailer is ready for download—I click a link, and in a few seconds the clip is playing. (It's amazing what you can learn about filmmaking from trailers, by the way; they're some of the best sources for how to present ideas and images in a short time span.) Sometimes the movie appears in a window in your Web browser, while other times the QuickTime Player plays the movie.

Exporting the Movie

The Export command lets you export a file in one of iMovie's common video sizes to the location of your choosing on disk (versus copying it to the iTunes library, for example).

Figure 17.1 Choose a destination and size to export the movie to disk.

To export the movie:

1. With the project selected in the Project List, choose Export Movie from the Share menu, or press Command-E.

2. In the dialog that appears, navigate to the location on your hard disk (**Figure 17.1**).

3. Select a size to export by clicking its radio button. (The dimensions of the sizes vary depending on whether you're exporting DV or high-definition footage.)

4. Click the Export button to create the movie.

✔ Tip

■ iMovie offers a handy estimate of how much space the exported movie will occupy on disk (**Figure 17.2**).

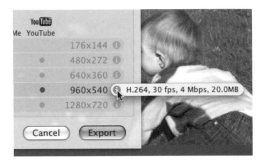

Figure 17.2 Move the mouse pointer over the "i" icon to view an estimate of the project's size when saved.

Exporting Windows-Friendly Movies

Want to send a movie file that a friend using Windows can read? iMovie can export a movie in the AVI format: choose Export Using QuickTime from the Share menu and, from the Export pop-up menu, choose Movie to AVI (see the next page for more details). You're likely to end up with a file that seems unnecessarily large. Instead, encourage your friend to install QuickTime (it's free), or you can use a utility such as HandBrake (handbrake.fr) to convert the file. Also check into Flip4Mac WMV (www.flip4mac.com) and Perian (perian.org) for additional video format plug-ins you can install for QuickTime.

Figure 17.3 Click the Options button in the Save dialog to access specific custom settings.

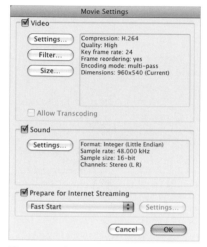

Figure 17.4 The Movie Settings dialog presents an overview of the current export settings.

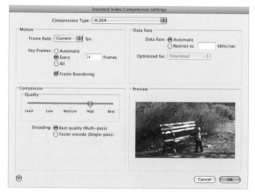

Figure 17.5 After that long progression of dialogs, you finally reach Compression Settings, where you can adjust the type and amount of compression used for exporting.

Exporting to QuickTime

iMovie's stock export settings are good for most situations, but you can also use other compression formats and options by way of QuickTime's Expert Settings.

To change image settings:

1. Select your project in the Project List.

2. Choose Export using QuickTime from the Share menu.

3. In the Save Exported File As dialog, make sure Movie to QuickTime Movie is selected in the Export pop-up menu, and click the Options button (**Figure 17.3**).

4. The Movie Settings dialog displays the current video and sound settings (**Figure 17.4**). To fine-tune the type and amount of video compression applied, click the Settings button under Video.

5. In the top area of the Compression Settings dialog, choose a compression method from the first pop-up menu (**Figure 17.5**). (Note that this dialog may look different depending on the compression type you're using. The option shown here is H.264.)

6. Move the Quality slider to the lowest level you can that maintains good image quality; the thumbnail shows you how much compression is being applied.

7. In the Motion area, select the number of frames per second from the Frame Rate pop-up menu.

continues on next page

8. Enter a number in the Key Frames Every [number] frames field to set how often a key frame is generated. Compression works by removing areas of a frame that have not changed since the preceding frame; to create a key frame, iMovie draws an entirely new frame.

9. To target a specific data rate, enter a value in the field labeled Restrict to [number] kbits/sec.

10. Click OK to return to Movie Settings.

11. Click OK to get back to the Save dialog, and then click the Save button to create the file.

To change audio settings:

1. Share your movie as described in the previous steps.

2. In the Sound portion of the Movie Settings dialog, click the Settings button to display sound-specific settings (**Figure 17.6**).

3. Choose a format from the Format pop-up menu. Some compressors include further settings, which are accessed by clicking the Show Advanced Settings checkbox. These usually determine how the data is encoded, or specify a data rate (or bit rate).

4. Decide whether the audio will play back in stereo or mono by choosing an option from the Channels pop-up menu. Stereo sounds better, but Mono offers a smaller file size.

5. In the Rate field, type a kHz value or select one from the pop-up menu to the right. Lower kHz settings will degrade the sound quality.

6. Click OK to exit the sound settings portion of the dialog.

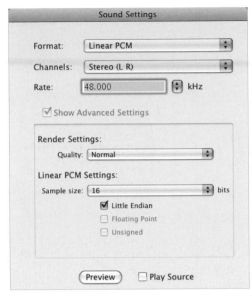

Figure 17.6 Choose an audio compressor to fine-tune how your movie's audio sounds after exporting.

QuickTime versus QuickTime Pro

Every Mac comes with QuickTime, including the free QuickTime Player, which allows you to play QuickTime movies and a host of other file formats (ranging from MPEG-formatted movies to MP3 audio files). If you're serious about optimizing your QuickTime movies for the Web, however, consider paying the $30 for a QuickTime Pro license, which turns QuickTime Player into a sophisticated movie editor. Not only does it give you an easy way to resize or recompress QuickTime movies, it also lets you save your movies into other formats, such as AVI, which Windows users can view if they don't have QuickTime installed.

Video Compression Terms You Should Know

Codec: Short for compression/decompression; another name for a compressor.

Compression: The method used to reduce the size of the movie file while still retaining image quality. Video and audio compression make for a tricky business. You have to weigh the benefits of smaller file sizes (and therefore potentially faster downloads) against the desire to have the best-looking movies possible. Many methods of compression are available, each with its own strengths. **Table 17.1** on the previous page provides an overview of the compressors available when exporting from iMovie. More are available if you export files from QuickTime Player Pro, and still more are offered by professional editing packages such as Apple's Compressor (part of Final Cut Studio) or Cleaner (`www.autodesk.com/cleaner`).

Data Rate: The amount of data sent from one point to another during a given time, such as the number of kilobytes delivered during a Web download.

Frame Rate: The number of frames displayed during 1 second. As more frames are included, the movie will play more smoothly—but adding frames increases the size of the file. Uncompressed DV video runs at 30 frames per second (fps) for NTSC, or 25 fps for PAL; a typical QuickTime movie contains 15 or 12 frames per second.

Key Frame: A complete movie frame that acts as the image base for successive frames. Unlike film, which displays 24 full frames per second on a reel of celluloid, QuickTime compares most of the frames in a movie with its key frames and notes the differences. Although this sounds like more work than just displaying each frame in its entirety, it actually means the movie player is drawing less data.

For example, consider a clip where the camera is stationary, filming a person talking. Every pixel of the first frame, the key frame, is drawn; in the next frame, the only change is that the person's lips have moved. Instead of redrawing the background and everything else, QuickTime holds onto the first frame and only changes the pixels around the person's mouth. So, the second frame (and third, fourth, and so on) contain only a few pixels' worth of information, dramatically reducing the total amount of data required and creating a smaller file. Of course, the entire movie likely won't be composed of just the person talking, so QuickTime creates several key frames along the way, allowing the player to regroup and start over. The more key frames that appear in your movie, the larger the file size will be.

Sample Rate: The quality of audio, measured in kilohertz (kHz). The higher the number, the more audio data is present, and therefore the better the quality of sound.

Table 17.1

QuickTime Video Compressors *

COMPRESSOR NAME	COMMENTS
Animation	Works best on computer-generated animations with broad areas of flat color. Doesn't work well for scenes with lots of color changes.
Apple VC.263	Originally designed for videoconferencing. Very high compression ratios. Sometimes good for Web video.
Apple Pixlet Video	A low file size format developed by Apple and Pixar for desktop editing of high-resolution footage.
DV-PAL, DV/DVCPRO-NTSC, DVCPRO-PAL, DVCPRO50-NTSC/PAL	Used by digital video cameras.
H.264	A high-quality, scalable video format included with QuickTime 7 (and available under Mac OS X 10.4 Tiger or later). H.264 is designed to run on devices as varied as cellular phones and high-definition televisions, and is the backbone of upcoming HD DVD formats.
JPEG 2000	High image quality and resolution for still images, using wavelet compression.
MPEG-4 Video	High quality compressed video based on QuickTime.
None	Good for capture only. Does almost no compression.
Photo-JPEG	Ideal for high-quality compressed still images. Also useful as an intermediate storage format for movies and QuickTime VR panoramas. Decompresses too slowly for video-based playback.
PNG	Typically used for still-image compression. Can get high compression ratios.

Note: The Minimum Install of QuickTime (which many users will choose) doesn't install all these compressors. If the computer being used to play a movie that requires one of these compressors has an Internet connection, QuickTime downloads the necessary compressor when it is needed for decompression.

* This table has been adapted from one that originally appeared in *QuickTime 5 for Macintosh and Windows: Visual QuickStart Guide*, by Judith Stern and Robert Lettieri, and is used here with their permission. (www.judyandrobert.com)

✔ Tips

■ The H.264 codec is mighty impressive, but it's also a resource hog, especially if you opt to use Multi-pass compression. It may take a while to export the file.

■ If you want to export only the audio portion of your movie, choose Sound to AIFF from the Export pop-up menu in the Save Exported File As dialog. Or, when you're in the Movie Settings dialog, deselect the Video checkbox before exporting.

■ If you're going to be exporting a lot of video, consider purchasing El Gato's Turbo.264 HD hardware encoder (www.elgato.com/turbo264). It's an H.264 encoding chip that pops into a USB port and can dramatically speed video encoding.

■ See **Table 17.1** for a summary of the video compressors included with QuickTime.

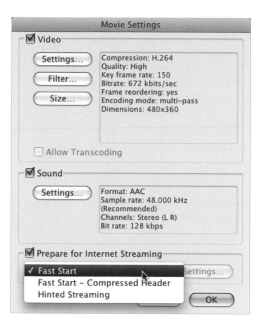

Figure 17.7 To enable Web streaming, click the Prepare for Internet Streaming box and choose a streaming method.

Figure 17.8 Preparing a QuickTime movie for streaming can get into a lot of geeky detail, but if you know what you're doing, you can improve streaming quality.

QuickTime Geekery

Trust me: Everything described so far in this chapter is really just the tip of a very large iceberg. If you're willing to shell out the bucks, software such as AutoDesk's Cleaner can encode and compress your movies into nearly any possible movie format, with more control than can be found in iMovie's or QuickTime Player's export features.

To prepare a movie for Internet streaming:

1. Share your movie as described in the previous steps.

2. In the Movie Settings dialog, click the Prepare for Internet Streaming box in the lower-left corner (**Figure 17.7**).

3. From the pop-up menu, select a streaming method:

   ▲ **Fast Start.** The movie file is downloaded like any other media file, and begins playing once enough data has been transferred.

   ▲ **Fast Start - Compressed Header.** Like Fast Start, the movie is downloaded as one file, but the header information is compressed to save disk space.

   ▲ **Hinted Streaming.** Use this option if the movie will be hosted by a QuickTime Streaming Server. Hinting the data breaks it into more manageable chunks for streaming. With Hinted Streaming selected, you can click the Settings button to further tweak the settings (**Figure 17.8**). For more information, see Apple's article: http://docs.info.apple.com/article.html?artnum=301355.

EXPORTING TO QUICKTIME

Exporting Final Cut XML

For some people, iMovie is just the first step in editing video. Because it's designed for building movies quickly, iMovie is often used to throw together a rough assembly; from there, the movie is sent to Final Cut Pro for refinement.

Rather than rely on Final Cut Pro to parse iMovie's file format, iMovie does the work ahead of time by creating an XML (eXtensible Markup Language) file compatible with Final Cut Pro. That file is a simple text file that tells Final Cut which edits are applied and where—you can open it in a text editor and see for yourself.

To export Final Cut XML:

1. Select the project you want to export in the Project List.

2. Choose Export Final Cut XML from the Share menu.

3. In the dialog that appears, choose a destination and enter a name for the XML file that will be created (**Figure 17.9**).

4. Click Save to build the XML file.

    After you import the file into Final Cut Pro, the video is ready for further editing (**Figure 17.10**).

✔ Tip

■ If you know you're going to end up in Final Cut Pro, don't bother making the movie pretty. All transitions are converted to the cross dissolves, audio not embedded in the video is ignored, and cropping and color adjustments also don't make the trip.

Figure 17.9 Create an XML file for Final Cut of your project that details all of the edits.

Figure 17.10 After importing the XML file into Final Cut Pro, your clips appear on the Timeline for editing.

MOVING FROM iMOVIE TO iDVD

18

My father had amassed a pretty large video-tape collection over several years. So you can imagine he did a fair bit of eye-rolling as DVD discs quickly gained in popularity, because that meant he needed to build a DVD collection, too.

DVD has several key advantages over VHS. The discs are smaller than videotapes, their image and sound quality are much better, and discs don't degrade over time (at least, not remotely as fast as tape, a fact you're no doubt aware of if you have an aging wedding or graduation video). And DVDs are inter-active: jump to your favorite scene in a movie; store several movies on one disc that can be accessed without fast-forwarding.

And yet, in Apple's eyes the DVD is already on its way out, expecting that soon everyone will be turning to the Web for distributing their movies. iMovie '08 removed a feature found in iMovie HD that let you create DVD chapter markers from within iMovie. That enabled you to set up chapters for the DVD.

Fortunately, the feature is back in iMovie '09, and is a breeze to use.

Creating Chapter Markers

When you watch a feature movie on DVD, you usually have the option of skipping to specific scenes, or chapters. You can set up chapter markers in iMovie that iDVD imports as chapters.

To set a chapter marker:

1. Make sure Show Advanced Tools is enabled in iMovie's preferences.

2. Click the Chapter Marker icon and drag it to a frame in your project (**Figure 18.1**).

    You can also Control-click (or right-click) a frame and choose Add Chapter Marker from the contextual menu.

3. Enter a name for the marker and press Return (**Figure 18.2**).

To relocate a chapter marker:

◆ Click and drag the marker elsewhere in the movie project.

To delete a chapter marker:

◆ Select the marker and press Delete.

To jump to a chapter marker:

◆ Click the triangle to the right of the marker icons and choose from the pop-up menu that appears (**Figure 18.3**).

To send the movie to iDVD:

◆ Choose iDVD from the Share menu. iMovie prepares the movie, opens iDVD, and creates a new project with the movie already loaded.

✔ Tip

■ Chapter markers, compared to comment markers, are a rust color with an arrow before the name. If your chapters aren't showing up, check the type of markers.

Chapter Marker

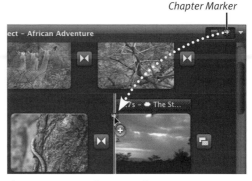

Figure 18.1 Drag a chapter marker to your movie to let viewers jump to that spot in the DVD.

Figure 18.2 Give your marker a name to locate it easily.

Figure 18.3 The pop-up menu near the marker icons lets you jump to those spots in your movie.

19

iDVD at a Glance

When the DVD format started gaining popularity in the 1990s, folks at home who wanted to watch the newest blockbusters on their couches weren't the only happy ones. Amateur and professional filmmakers finally had an easy, nearly-universal way to share their movies with other people. DVDs were small, they stored a huge amount of data (4.7 gigabytes!), and offered the ability to skip ahead to selected scenes.

Except it wasn't easy to get your movie onto one of these shiny platters. The DVD specification is quite particular about where and how files are stored.

When Apple introduced iDVD, all the fuss fell by the wayside. You brought your movie into iDVD, spent some time customizing the look, and burned a disc that could play in a standard DVD player.

Now, with broadband Internet gaining acceptance, there isn't as much interest in DVDs—especially by Apple, which barely updated iDVD for iLife '09.

Still, it's easier to burn a disc and mail it off to the grandparents. This chapter provides an overview of how it's done (and be sure to read the sidebar at left).

Download the iDVD Section of This Book for Free!

When Apple released iLife '09, the company added a lot of new features to iMovie but barely touched iDVD. To keep this book from becoming a 500-page behemoth, I decided to pull the bulk of the iDVD section and offer it as a free download.

This chapter and the next cover the basics of creating and burning a DVD using iDVD, but there's much more to the program. The free chapters detail how to use features such as OneStep DVD and Magic iDVD, work with submenus, customize themes, change backgrounds and buttons, and more.

Visit http://jeffcarlson.com/imovievqs/ to register this book and download the PDF.

iDVD at a Glance

With your iMovie project shared to iDVD, most of the work is done. In fact, if you wanted you could just burn a disc right now.

However, you probably want to do a little customization before making the disc. Here's an overview of the process.

Themes

iDVD applies its first theme to your project (**Figure 19.1**), but you can choose another. Several themes include one or more *drop zones*, areas that display a preview of your movie or other media you choose.

To choose a theme:

1. Click a different theme icon in the Themes pane; the pop-up menu at the top of the pane reveals many more themes.

2. If your project is in standard (4:3) format, iDVD asks if you'd like to use the widescreen (16:9) version of the theme; click Keep to leave the aspect ratio as-is, or click Change to apply the widescreen version.

3. In the Apply Theme Family dialog that appears, click OK to apply the theme to all menus in the project.

   The new theme is applied (**Figure 19.2**).

To add media to drop zones:

1. Click the Media button to reveal the Media pane.

2. Click the Edit Drop Zones button to view the drop zones available for the theme.

3. Drag a photo or movie from the Media pane to a drop zone (**Figure 19.3**).

   You can also drag to a drop zone within the main screen itself.

Figure 19.1 iDVD applies a theme to your project.

Figure 19.2 Choose a new theme in the pane at right.

Edit Drop Zones button

Figure 19.3 Drag photos or movies onto drop zones.

Autoplay well   DVD Map button

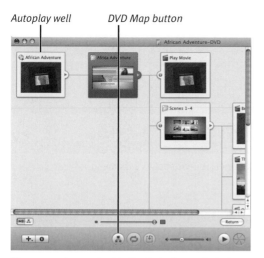

Figure 19.4 Any content in the Autoplay well starts automatically when the DVD is played.

Figure 19.5 Drag the movie out of the Autoplay well to disable the autoplay feature.

The Autoplay well

Although iDVD in iLife '09 remains largely untouched from the previous version, there is one important change. Projects shared from iMovie automatically appear in the Autoplay well, a special area of iDVD's project map. When you insert a disc into a DVD player, your movie starts playing immediately, even before the main menu appears.

Apple implemented this feature so that people could quickly burn an iMovie project to disc and not deal with setting themes or other iDVD features. If you want your viewers to see the main menu first, follow these steps.

To disable the Autoplay movie:

1. Click the DVD Map button to display your project's structure (**Figure 19.4**).

2. Drag the movie out of the Autoplay well to remove it (you're not deleting the movie from the project). The movie disappears in a puff of smoke (**Figure 19.5**).

3. Click the Return button to go back to the main menu. Now, when the burned disc is played, the first thing the viewer sees will be the menu, not the movie.

Important iDVD Interface Terms

◆ **Button.** Any interactive element in the DVD workspace is a *button*, even if it doesn't always look like a button. New movies, slideshows, and chapters are all buttons, because they require some sort of action on the part of the user to activate them.

◆ **Submenu.** The exception to buttons are *submenus*, which are containers that hold more stuff. An example of a submenu would be the "Scene Selection" option that appears when you import a movie with chapter markers. The item is a control that takes you to another menu screen, which includes buttons for each chapter that you've set.

◆ **Theme.** A *theme* is the overall look of a menu screen, including the visual presentation (fonts, colors, etc.) as well as the way it interacts (with motion menus, etc.).

Slideshows

You're not limited to including just the movie you created in iMovie on your disc. iDVD can build photo slideshows so you can show off still pictures as well.

To create a slideshow:

1. Click the Add button and choose Add slideshow from the pop-up menu that appears (**Figure 19.6**). A new item appears called My Slideshow.

2. Double-click the My Slideshow button to open the Slideshow editor.

3. Drag photos from the Media pane to the editor (**Figure 19.7**).

4. Click the Return button to go back to the main menu.

To preview the project:

◆ Click the Preview button in the lower-right corner of the window. The iDVD interface changes to show a preview of the DVD, complete with a remote control that lets you simulate how the disc will appear (**Figure 19.8**). Click the Exit button on the remote to return to iDVD's editing environment.

✔ Tip

■ As this book went to press, iDVD has a bug where the name of your iMovie project doesn't transfer to iDVD. So although the filename matches the project, the title on the main menu reads "iMovie Project." To change the title, double-click it and type a new one.

Figure 19.6 Add a photo slideshow to your disc.

Figure 19.7 Arrange photos in the Slideshow editor.

Figure 19.8 Use the preview feature to see how the DVD will operate once it's burned.

ARCHIVING, ENCODING, AND BURNING

20

iMovie's purpose is to create a movie, which can be published to a Web page, sent to an iPod or Apple TV, or distributed in other ways. iDVD's purpose, however, is to create a project that can be burned to a DVD disc. It contains high-quality video and audio that will play on a consumer DVD player. Without the disc-burning step, iDVD is pretty much just an interesting exercise in customizing a user interface.

True to form, the process of burning a disc is simple: click the glowing Burn button, insert a recordable DVD disc (DVD-R, DVD-RW, DVD+R, or DVD+RW), and go outside to enjoy the sunshine for a few hours. But getting to that point, while not difficult, involves a few choices that determine the amount of data that can be stored on the disc and the quality of the finished project.

Creating a Project Archive

Burning a DVD takes a lot of hard disk space and processing power. Some people choose to build a project using one Mac (such as a laptop), and then burn the DVD on another computer (such as a desktop Mac, which boasts a faster processor). Or, perhaps your Mac doesn't include a SuperDrive. In these situations, create an archive of your project that can be copied to another machine.

If you're planning to burn a disc on your computer but don't need an archive, skip ahead to "Choosing an Encoding Setting."

To create a project archive:

1. Choose Archive Project from the File menu. If your project isn't saved, iDVD asks you to save it. To continue, click OK in the dialog that appears; otherwise, click Cancel.

2. In the Save As dialog that appears, choose a location for the archive and, optionally, change its name (**Figure 20.1**).

3. Enable or disable the following options. The estimated size of the archive appears to the right and changes based on your choices.

   ▲ **Include themes.** If your project uses themes that aren't likely to be on another computer (such as third-party themes you purchased, or favorite themes you designed), enable this option to copy the necessary information to the archive. If you leave this disabled, but your project contains custom elements, an error dialog appears on the other computer when you open the archive (**Figure 20.2**).

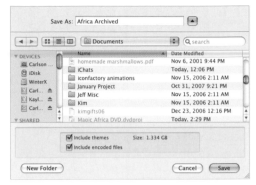

Figure 20.1 When you save your project as an archive, the Save As dialog contains archive-specific options.

Figure 20.2 Choose Include themes when saving an archive to avoid an error dialog like this one.

External Burners

For most of iDVD's existence, the only official way to burn a DVD was to do it on a Mac that contained an Apple-supplied internal SuperDrive. Now, at long last, that restriction is history: you can burn to external DVD burners directly from iDVD.

Figure 20.3 If you have protected audio files in your project, you need to authorize the computer with your iTunes Music Store ID and password.

Figure 20.4 An archive is significantly larger than an iDVD project file because it stores all of the media, rather than including just pointers to the data.

▲ **Include encoded files.** iDVD can encode material in the background, which reduces the time it takes to burn the disc (see "Choosing an Encoding Setting" on the next page). Including these files means it will take less time to burn the project on another machine, but it also makes the archive size larger.

4. Click Save. After a few minutes, depending on the size of your project, a new archive file is created.

✔ Tips

■ An archive contains all the data your project needs—except fonts. If your project contains a font that may not be on the computer to which you're sending the archive, be sure to also send a copy of the font.

■ If you've included any protected audio files (such as older songs purchased from the iTunes Music Store) in your archive, you won't be able to open the project on another computer unless that machine is authorized by you. A warning dialog appears (**Figure 20.3**), and then opens iTunes so you can input your iTunes Music Store identification and password.

■ So why not just copy the project file? To save disk space while you're working, iDVD includes pointers to the media and other data in your project, not the data itself. Copying just the project file to another machine wouldn't include that information. An archive packs it all into a nice tidy package (**Figure 20.4**).

Choosing an Encoding Setting

iDVD employs three encoding methods: Best Performance, High Quality, and Professional Quality.

To choose an encoding setting for the current project:

1. Choose Project Info from the Project menu or press Command-I.

2. Choose an option from the Encoding popup menu (**Figure 20.5**).

To choose an encoding setting for new projects:

1. Open iDVD's preferences and click the Projects icon.

2. For the Encoding setting, click the radio button beside the type of encoding you wish to use.

Best Performance

Best Performance provides up to 60 minutes of video and shorter burn times than High Quality. iDVD encodes the video while it's running, whether you're doing something else in iDVD or working in another program (**Figure 20.6**).

High Quality

If your project exceeds 60 minutes, or you want to make sure you're getting a higher quality encoding than Best Performance, use the High Quality mode. After you start the burn process, iDVD examines the video to determine where it can apply different levels of compression (a process called Variable Bitrate, or VBR, encoding).

Figure 20.5 The encoding options are located in the Project Info window, as well as in iDVD's preferences.

Figure 20.6 With the Best Performance setting enabled, iDVD encodes movies in the background. The Project Info window reports on the progress.

Figure 20.7 Professional Quality projects tend to producer richer color fidelity.

Encoding and Burn Times

To give you a rough idea of how long it takes for iDVD to encode projects using the encoding settings, here are the results of burning a two-hour project on a 2.4 GHz iMac.

High Quality: 1 hours 15 minutes.
Professional Quality: 3 hours 52 minutes.

High Quality

Best Performance

High Quality

Best Performance

Figure 20.8 These examples come from a 118-minute project (High Quality) and the same footage in a 48-minute project (Best Performance). More motion and noise gets more compression (top), resulting in pixelation around the trees (detail). However, when there is less motion, the two encoding styles look very much alike (bottom, with detail).

Professional Quality

Professional Quality uses the same encoding algorithms found in Apple's pro-level applications. Like High Quality, it uses VBR, but it takes two passes through the footage to optimize the compression. Professional Quality projects tend to feature richer colors and better reproduction than High Quality projects (**Figure 20.7**).

✔ Tips

- If you're using Best Performance, wait until the assets are finished encoding in the Project Info window before you burn.

- High and Professional Quality do not encode video in the background the way Best Performance does. Instead, they perform calculations during the burning phase. So, don't stare at the Encoding area waiting for the encoding to finish, because it hasn't started.

- As projects get longer than 60 minutes, their image quality is more likely to decrease due to the additional compression that needs to be applied. If higher image quality is important to you, try not to skirt that two-hour border with your project sizes (**Figure 20.8**).

- After you burn a project using High or Professional Quality, iDVD holds onto the files it encoded. However, if you remove any assets from the project and want to burn it again, be sure to first choose Delete Encoded Assets from the Advanced menu to force iDVD to re-scan the footage and choose the best compression settings.

- The Capacity figure in the Project Info window is based on the type of encoding you've specified. If iDVD is set to use Best Performance but the capacity exceeds 4.2 GB, switch to High or Professional Quality—iDVD changes its estimate.

Burning the DVD

Before you click the Burn button, make sure you have enough hard disk space available: at least twice the amount the project occupies. You can view your project's size and the free space on the hard disk that contains your project by choosing Project Info from the Project menu.

To change the name of the burned disc:

1. Choose Project Info from the Project menu, or press Command-I. The Project Info window appears (**Figure 20.9**).

2. Type a new name in the Disc Name field. After the disc is burned, this name is used when the DVD is mounted on a computer's desktop.

3. Close the window to apply the change.

To locate a missing asset:

1. Choose Project Info from the Project menu, or press Command-I to display the Project Info window.

2. Scroll through the asset list to find entries with a zero (**0**) in the Status column (**Figure 20.10**).

3. Double-click the missing asset to bring up the Missing Files dialog.

4. Select a file in the dialog and click the Find File button.

5. Locate the file and press OK. The Status column displays a checkmark. Note that for missing imported videos, you need to re-link the video and audio portions (just point to the same file).

6. Click OK to exit the dialog.

Figure 20.9 In the Project Info window, change the name of the disc when it's inserted in a computer.

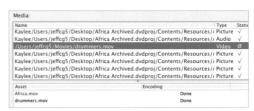

Figure 20.10 Use the Project Info window to locate missing assets.

How to Fix Missing Assets

The Project Info dialog tracks everything you've added to the project, even assets that you've deleted. If the file cannot be found, iDVD will not proceed when the time comes to burn.

I learned this the hard way when I dragged a JPEG image file to a menu background, decided it didn't look good, and then deleted it from the Background well in the Menu pane. Since the image no longer appeared in the project, I deleted it from my hard disk.

There are two solutions:

◆ Double-click the item in the Project Info window and choose another image.

◆ Go to the Map view and delete the asset entirely.

BURNING THE DVD

Normal   *Activated*

Figure 20.11 You need to click the Burn button only once to start the process (some earlier versions required two clicks). So, really, there's no good reason to hide the button behind the safety iris—except that it's cool.

Figure 20.12 If errors are found before burning, iDVD gives you the opportunity to fix or ignore them.

In the Map view, position your mouse pointer over a warning icon to locate potential burn problems.

Figure 20.13 The disc burning process goes through five stages of encoding and writing data to disc. The small preview helps you determine how far along the process has advanced.

To burn the DVD:

1. Click the Burn button; the iris reveals the glowing Burn button that's been hiding under iDVD's interface (**Figure 20.11**).

   If any assets are missing, iDVD displays a warning dialog (**Figure 20.12**). The Map view also displays potential burn problems.

   (The "closed" Burn button is like the bright red safety cover that's always mounted over The Big Important Button—the one that launches the missiles, opens the airlocks, or initiates the self-destruct sequence that destroys the villian's secret underground lair in all those movies.)

   Otherwise, the program asks you to insert a blank recordable DVD disc.

2. A progress dialog appears that identifies the stages of the process (**Figure 20.13**):

   ▲ **Stage 1: Prepare.** iDVD ensures that it has everything it needs to continue burning.

   ▲ **Stage 2: Process Menus.** Buttons, motion menus, and other menu interface elements are rendered and encoded.

   ▲ **Stage 3: Process Slideshows.** Slideshow photos are resized and compressed as needed. If you've specified slideshow transitions, they are rendered separately during this stage.

   ▲ **Stage 4: Process Movies.** Depending on which encoding method you've chosen, this stage usually takes the longest.

   ▲ **Stage 5: Burn.** The footage is *multiplexed*, which combines the audio and video data into a single stream that can be read by DVD players. Burning is when the laser actually etches your data into the surface of the disc.

BURNING THE DVD

✔ Tips

- If you've specified Best Performance, wait for asset encoding to finish before starting the burn process.

- Remember that the total space occupied on the disc includes motion menus, slideshows, etc. So if your movie is 56 minutes long, you may still get an error message that the project is too big.

- Earlier versions of iDVD required you to enable the Motion button to include motion on the disc, but iDVD now renders the motion elements whether the Motion button is highlighted or not. To burn a project with no motion, set the Loop Duration slider in the Menu Info window to zero (00:00).

- I frequently burn test copies of a project to a rewriteable DVD-RW disc, so I'm not throwing away a bunch of shiny platters. When you insert such a disc that already has data on it, iDVD gives you the option to erase it before continuing with the burn process (**Figure 20.14**).

- Including transitions between menus or within slideshows adds time to the burning process.

- Did you create a widescreen movie in iMovie, but it's not appearing as widescreen in your DVD player? Check to see if the player has a 16:9 or letterbox feature. Some models (such as mine at home) play the movie full frame if it doesn't detect a flag on the disc instructing it to letterbox the picture.

- Wondering at what speed your Super-Drive is burning the disc? The answer is found in Mac OS X's console.log file. After you burn a project, open the file, located at [Computer]/Library/Logs/Console/.

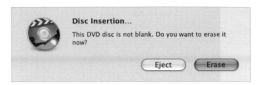

Figure 20.14 If you insert a rewriteable disc that contains data, iDVD can erase it during the burn stage.

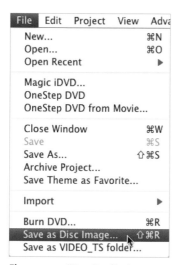

Figure 20.15 "Burn" a disc image to your hard drive.

Figure 20.16 Drag a disc image to Disk Utility to burn its contents to a DVD disc.

Save as VIDEO_TS Folder

If you just want to test the quality of the encoded material on the same machine, choose Save as VIDEO_TS folder from the File menu. This option does the same work as creating a disc image, but the files are just stored in a folder (and therefore are not as transportable). Point DVD Player at that folder to watch the "disc."

Saving as a Disc Image

Until iDVD 5, you needed to own a Mac with an Apple-supplied SuperDrive to burn iDVD projects. It wouldn't work with third-party external burners.

Now, that restriction is gone. However, there are still occasions when you want to save the project as a disc image, which effectively "burns" your project to the hard drive. For example, you may want to burn a DVD disc from that disc image on another computer, or mount the image on your desktop and preview the final project using the DVD Player application.

To save as a disc image:

1. Instead of clicking the Burn button, choose Save As Disc Image from the File menu, or press Command-Shift-R (**Figure 20.15**).

2. Choose a location on your hard disk to save the disc image; make sure you have plenty of free space.

3. Click the Save button. iDVD follows the same procedure as when it burns a disc.

To burn a DVD disc from a disc image:

1. Launch Disk Utility (located in Applications > Utilities).

2. Drag the disc image from the Finder to the left-hand column (**Figure 20.16**); or, choose Open from the Images menu.

3. Select the disc image in Disk Utility and click the Burn button.

4. Insert a recordable disc.

To play a disc image using DVD Player:

1. Double-click the disc image to mount the disc as if it were a physical DVD.

2. Launch the DVD Player application.

SAVING AS A DISC IMAGE

After the Burn

When the burning process is complete, iDVD spits out the DVD disc and asks if you'd like to make another copy (**Figure 20.17**). If so, insert a new disc; otherwise, click Done.

Here are a few other suggested things to do while you're in your cooling down period.

Test your project

Just because you have a shiny disc in hand doesn't guarantee that it works. Test it on your own machine using DVD Player. Test it on friends' Macs and PCs, and insert it in your consumer DVD player. Test, test, test, or you may find yourself singing, "To every season, burn, burn, burn...".

Delete encoded assets

If you don't need to burn another disc, you can free up some hard disk space by deleting the project's encoded assets, which are stored in the project file.

Create an archive of the project for offline storage to make sure you have all of the original footage.

To delete encoded assets:

◆ From the Advanced menu, choose Delete Encoded Assets.

Make duplicates

If you want to make copies of the DVD without going through the iDVD burning process, use Disk Utility or other software such as Roxio's Toast (`www.roxio.com`).

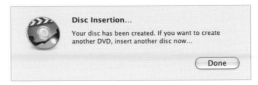

Figure 20.17 If you're creating multiple copies of the same disc, burn them in succession so you don't have to go through the encoding stage each time.

TROUBLESHOOTING

My first bit of troubleshooting advice is to make sure you're running the latest versions of iMovie and iDVD; check the iLife page at Apple's Web site (`www.apple.com/ilife/`) or run Software Update (in your System Preferences or from the Apple menu).

Also, check Apple's online support discussion forums for iMovie and iDVD (`discussions.info.apple.com`) to see if other users have found solutions or workarounds to a problem you may be experiencing. I owe a great debt to many folks online who have prodded the programs to find answers.

Finally—and perhaps most important—*give Apple feedback* (`www.apple.com/feedback`). It's the best way to communicate what needs fixing (and yes, the developers do listen).

iMovie and iDVD Troubleshooting

iMovie seems to prefer lots of memory and fast processors, but even on powerful Macs you might see sluggish behavior. Try the following suggestions to improve performance.

Make the iMovie window smaller

Use the resize handle on the bottom-right corner of the iMovie window to make it as small as it will go.

Quit other running applications

This frees up more memory for iMovie to use. Although Mac OS X manages memory better than Mac OS 9, I've seen iMovie and iDVD gain some pep if they're not competing with other processes.

Defragment your hard disk

You can run into performance issues if your hard disk space is severely fragmented—there aren't enough open stretches of disk space available to write entire files, so the files are broken up into pieces to fit the available free locations.

The best way to defragment a disk is to make a complete backup copy of it, erase the drive, and then restore the data.

Turn off FileVault

FileVault is a technology introduced in Mac OS X 10.3 that creates an encrypted version of your Home directory. However, iDVD and iMovie store their project files in the Home directory, which means that when FileVault is active, the computer is constantly encrypting and decrypting massive quantities of data on the fly. Turn it off in Mac OS X's Security preference pane.

Trash iMovie or iDVD preferences

If the program's preferences get corrupted, it places a load on the program's operation. iMovie and iDVD re-create the files they need the next time you launch the program.

To trash iMovie or iDVD preferences:

1. Quit the application.

2. Go to your preferences folder at [Home]/Library/Preferences/, and delete the following files (you may not have all of the iMovie files):
   ▲ iMovie Preferences
   ▲ com.apple.imovie.plist
   ▲ com.apple.iMovie7.plist
   ▲ com.apple.iMovie8.plist
   ▲ com.apple.iDVD.plist

Fixing out of sync audio/video

If your audio and video are out of sync in a video clip, make sure your audio was recorded at 16-bit, not 12-bit. See the following article for more information: http://docs.info.apple.com/article.html?artnum=61636.

Consult Apple's support pages

Apple publishes technotes about common issues and workarounds: www.apple.com/support/imovie/ and www.apple.com/support/idvd/.

Disc Burning

Here are some things to check if your discs are turning into drink coasters (or if you're not even getting to the burn stage).

Have lots of disk space

Make sure you have plenty of hard disk space available. Figure at least twice the size of your iDVD project as being a good starting point. You may have to copy your project to another disk (such as an external FireWire drive) and run it from there; iDVD stores its working files and encoded media within the project file, so even if you have a drive with lots of free space, iDVD will ignore it if the project file is not located there.

Ensure disk is formatted correctly

If you're using an external drive, make sure it's formatted as a Mac OS Extended (Journaled) volume. Some drives are pre-formatted for Windows or Unix operating systems, and although the Mac can read and write to them, iMovie and iDVD need to use Mac OS Extended (Journaled). Use Disk Utility to erase and reformat the drive.

Delete encoded assets

Some previously-encoded material could be causing problems. From iDVD's Advanced menu, choose Delete Encoded Assets, which deletes any rendered footage and forces iDVD to re-encode the material from scratch.

Check DVD media

Unfortunately, sometimes the problem is the blank DVD disc you're trying to burn onto. This can happen with less expensive discs purchased in bulk, but has been known to affect reputable manufacturers' discs, too. If you're getting errors, try a new media brand.

Clean your SuperDrive

A tiny laser burns pits into a disc, resulting in data that a computer or DVD player can read. If your SuperDrive has accumulated dust, it can throw off the beam and ruin your burn. Spray a little compressed air into the slot (but don't go crazy with it).

Set Energy Saver settings

Disc burning is processor-intensive. Go to the Energy Saver preference panel in Mac OS X's System Preferences and set the processor performance to Highest and the hard drive to never spin down. Also make sure that the computer won't go to sleep after a period of inactivity.

Burn during the day

It's convenient to start a burn late at night so the process will complete while you're sleeping. However, Mac OS X performs some nightly system maintenance at approximately 3 a.m., which can interfere with burn performance. Burn your project during the day to see if this is the culprit.

Change audio quality

iMovie and iDVD use audio set to 48.000 kHz (16-bit). However, some audio sources may record at 44.100 kHz, which has been known to cause burning problems.

To change a movie's audio quality:

1. Export your movie from iMovie to a QuickTime file using Expert Settings.

2. In the Movie Settings dialog, under Sound options, click the Settings button.

3. Click the Rate popup menu and choose 48.000.

4. Export the clip, then import it into iDVD.

INDEX

INDEX

INDEX

INDEX

INDEX